I0818977

The
Tupperware
Cookbook

The Tupperware Cookbook

OVER 100 MAKE-AHEAD RECIPES
with Low Waste and High Flavor

Authored with
THERESA GAMBACORTA

Photography by
EVA KOLENKO

TEN SPEED PRESS
California | New York

Tupperware

Contents

"With the right tools, I've developed a passion for cooking and having fun in the kitchen."

—MARIE-PIER T.,
11 YEARS SELLING TUPPERWARE PRODUCTS

CHAPTER THREE

Weeknight Winners 85

CHAPTER FOUR

Veggie Power 125

WELCOME TO *THE TUPPERWARE COOKBOOK*.

The story of Tupperware begins in the years after World War II. This was a time when American families were adapting to a new way of life—a strong postwar economy led to middle-class growth, and suburban living was on the rise. Americans suddenly had larger homes, plus more money, so they could take advantage of the latest technological advances. This was also the age of refrigerators, which replaced the need for inefficient ice boxes. Homemakers could cook ahead and store their leftovers and ingredients more easily than ever before. But food storage options were limited.

Enter Earl Tupper, a chemist and inventor at DuPont who saw an opportunity. He transformed

humble discarded material into a lightweight, durable bowl with a magic seal. Inspired by the tight closure of a paint can, he designed an airtight lid that, with a signature "burp," expelled air and locked in freshness (now known as the famous Tupperware Seal).

In 1946, his invention—called the Wonderlier Bowl—debuted in retail stores, offering a completely new way to keep food fresh. Yet for all its innovation, it didn't fly off the shelves. Shoppers were accustomed to glass and ceramic—plastic, even innovative plastic, was foreign.

Brownie Wise changed that. A single mother in Detroit with an entrepreneurial spirit and a gift for storytelling, she introduced a new

> "Brownie Wise's mission was to build the people and they will build the business. The Tupperware community has allowed me to build myself into a stronger person inside and out."
>
> —**KENDRA S.,**
> **4 YEARS SELLING TUPPERWARE PRODUCTS**

way to sell: the Tupperware party. It was simple but revolutionary. Friends and neighbors gathered to see the products firsthand—not just as buyers but as part of a community. Instead of retail purchases, Tupperware parties and direct sales became the *only* way to buy Tupperware products.

By 1951, Earl Tupper saw Wise's impact and brought her on as vice president of marketing, making her one of the first women to hold such a high-ranking corporate position in the United States. Under her leadership, the home-party model exploded in popularity, spreading across North America and beyond.

For many today, the words *Tupperware party* invoke visions of retro gatherings where women—mostly homemakers—would meet to chat, snack, and take a look at the latest Tupperware product release. Who could forget their parents' beloved avocado-green Tupperware bowl with the sunburst lid? Or the family Cake Taker, which frequently transported decadent desserts to parties and school bake sales? And, of course, there was the ever-present CHIP 'N DIP set.

These parties were a chance to trade kitchen secrets over cookies and punch and to bond with friends and neighbors, but there was also something more powerful at work: These gatherings offered ways for our mothers and grandmothers to contribute to their families with extra income. And for women in the years after World War II, the ability to tap into their entrepreneurial spirit was particularly powerful. Throughout the 1960s and '70s, women across the world—many with limited access to means of earning income—used this model to build businesses of their own.

And it's that path that leads us to the present. For generations, the Tupperware brand has been more than just a collection of products. It has been a symbol of quality, innovation, connection, and opportunity—an enduring cultural icon that has shaped how families conserve food, how communities gather, and how women create their own opportunities. Today, we're finding new ways to bring Tupperware products into the modern kitchen—saving money and time, and creating a library of healthy, make-ahead, low-waste recipes to cook and eat with your family, friends, or just on your own.

The recipes in this book take inspiration in part from the early days of Tupperware parties—from the smart prep, ingenious food hacks, and clever kitchen know-how passed down through generations, with an emphasis on spending less time in the kitchen and bringing joy by sharing and gathering (and more time around a CHIP 'N DIP set!). The recipes also look to the future: for harried parents, busy career men and women, vibrant party throwers, eco-conscious and veg-forward alike. Because in the end, great meals are more than just about what's on the plate. They're about the experiences, traditions, and memories they create. Welcome to the Tupperware kitchen!

1/2 cup

Tupperware Kitchen Essentials

You can make the recipes in this book with everyday kitchen equipment and tools you probably already have on hand. However, there is a bevy of Tupperware tools designed to ease your workload, speed up meal prep, and make your dishes shine. Here's a list of some of the most often used innovative, energy-efficient, lightweight, and space-saving tools.

ALL-IN-ONE SHAKER

For anything that needs a quick shake—from batters and dressings to shakes, marinades, and more—this is a great multitasker, with no electricity or sharp blending gear required. The nifty measurements help keep everything precise.

Replaces: Measuring cup and whisk

FREEZER MATES

Super sustainable and stackable, these handy containers have a stain-resistant coating, so even the most vibrant curry, sauce, or marinade won't leave its mark on them. And an innovative lid helps ward off any ice build-up, which makes these a meal prepper's best friend.

Replaces: Single-use plastic freezer bags

FRIDGESMART CONTAINERS

Storing your fresh fruits and vegetables in these containers keeps them as fresh as the day you bought them—potentially for up to three full weeks, thanks to an innovative three-way vent system that maintains the atmosphere inside the container by balancing the flow of oxygen coming in and carbon dioxide going out.

Replaces: Single-use plastic bags

GRATE N STORE

From shredded potatoes to all sorts of cheeses and more, you can neatly and efficiently prepare your ingredients in advance using this tool and store them in the same container: just rotate the handle clockwise for fine grating and counterclockwise for coarse.

Replaces: Box grater and storage containers

JEL-RING MOLD

Effortlessly craft stunning gelatin desserts, no-bake cheesecakes, and frozen treats with this classic mold. The smooth interior and removable insert ensure easy, mess-free unmolding, and the airtight lid keeps your creations fresh until ready to serve.

Replaces: Metal Bundt pans, disposable pans

MANDOLINE

This adjustable mandoline, which comes with multiple blades, makes slicing and julienning vegetables quick, safe, and precise. The hand-guard protects fingers, while the sharp blades deliver uniform cuts every time. Ideal for thinly slicing and julienning vegetables for salads.

Replaces: Paring knife, chef's knife, and traditional mandoline

MEASURING MATES

Traditional sets of measuring cups and spoons come in only four sizes each, but this set provides cups and spoons in six sizes, which makes measuring ingredients faster and more efficient. Plus, the measurements are embedded on the handles, so they are easy to see and won't fade away after repeated washing.

Replaces: Measuring cups and spoons

MICRO PITCHER 2-PIECE SET

This two-piece set of handy, microwave-safe measuring pitchers is handy for melting butter, chocolate, and other melty delights with zero mess. You can use the pitchers separately, or you can place the smaller pitcher upside down on top of the larger pitcher to create a "lid" to keep your microwave clean.

Replaces: Liquid measuring cups and double boiler

MICROPRO SERIES GRILL

Craving something toasty but you don't want to drag out a bag of charcoal and fire up the grill? This specially designed "grill" is the answer. It converts microwaves to thermal heat—giving you a seared, low-mess meal—panini, burgers, fish, chicken, veggies, and more—in just minutes.

Replaces: Stovetop grill pan, conventional oven, skillet, and outdoor grill

MICROWAVE PASTA MAKER

No more waiting for water to boil with this helpful tool: simply add your pasta and water, using the handy measurement fill lines inside the base, and let the microwave do the work. When combined with the cover, the base doubles as a strainer, eliminating the need for a bulky colander. To keep mealtime even more low mess, serve the pasta directly from the Microwave Pasta Maker, then cover the base and store any leftovers in the fridge.

Replaces: Stockpot and colander or strainer

MICROWAVE RICE MAKER

Add rice or other grain to the base of this cooker, rinse and drain using the insert as a strainer, and then fill with cold water, cover, and cook in the microwave worry-free. The overflow guard insert prevents spills, while the handles make opening effortless.

Replaces: Electric rice cooker

ONE TOUCH FRESH CONTAINERS

Seal it, trust it! These airtight, stackable containers with effortless press-to-seal lids keep your meals and ingredients fresh, visible, and ready when you need them. Perfect for pantry staples, leftovers, or prepped ingredients, they come in multiple sizes.

Replaces: Single-use plastic bags

PORTIONING SCOOPS

A scooper meets a measuring spoon! A universal handle with three heavy-duty, snap-on scoops in different sizes, this space-saving tool works great for a variety of ingredients.

Small scoop = 1 tablespoon

Medium scoop = 2 tablespoons

Large scoop = 3¾ tablespoons

Replaces: Metal portioning scoops

SIFT 'N STORE

The Sift 'N Store tool simplifies any baking task that requires sifting, from dusting powdered sugar on top of cookies to mixing together fine flours and more. It has a funnel-shaped opening for easy refilling and top and bottom lids for convenient storage.

Replaces: Standard sifters

SILICONE BAKING FORMS

These handy baking forms are super easy to unmold even the most stubborn of bakes, no greasing required. Perfect for a mix of recipes, these molds are oven, microwave, freezer, and dishwasher-safe.

Replaces: Parchment, foil, and paper liners

SILICONE SPATULA

This spatula is perfect for folding fluffy batters, scraping sticky caramel, and stirring warm sauces without threat of melting or warping. It also helps you use every last bit of food—whether it's batter from a bowl, a sauce from a pan, or a spread from a jar—so nothing goes to waste.

Replaces: Plastic spatula

SMART MULTI-COOKER

Innovation meets convenience with this three-in-one microwave cooker. Its shielded colander blocks microwaves from directly heating your food, allowing only the water below to boil, creating true steam cooking—preserving nutrients, flavor, and texture. Effortlessly steam vegetables, cook grains, or prepare pasta in one compact system, saving you time, effort, and storage space.

Replaces: Steamer, electric rice cooker

SNACK CUPS

Airtight and leak-proof, these handy containers let you easily take single servings of snacks, spices, small portions, and dressings anywhere or store at home in your pantry or fridge.

Replaces: Storage containers

SUPERSONIC CHOPPERS

These pull-cord choppers are perfect for dicing up large amounts of ingredients like garlic, onions, and herbs. But with just a few pulls of the cord, you can mix up a bevy of meals like pancake and cake batters, compound butter, hummus, graham cracker crusts, and more. Best of all, there's no electricity needed, and the non-slip base keeps the unit steady and quiet. Take one camping!

Replaces: Food processor

THATSA BOWL

Take your food prep to the next level! Designed for ease and control, the built-in thumb handle provides a secure grip whether you're mixing on a flat surface or holding the bowl close to your body. The textured interior helps minimize unsightly scratches, keeping this versatile bowl looking great over time.

Replaces: Mixing bowl

ULTIMATE SILICONE BAGS

This eco-friendly solution is a multitasker's dream: store food in the freezer, pack your lunch to go, reheat in the microwave, cook in the oven, and stash treats. Going on a picnic? Fill larger-size bags with water and freeze the night before and you'll have ice packs for your cooler to keep your lunch cool.

Replaces: Single-use plastic bags and containers

WHIP 'N MIX CHEF

With this cordless multipurpose mixer, you can whip cream until light and fluffy, mix heavy batters, or use the funnel for slowly adding liquids to make homemade dressing. Simplify baking and save bowls by mixing thick batters for muffins and cakes in the base. This handy multitasker is compact, efficient, and dishwasher-safe, making it ideal for tight spaces and busy people living.

Replaces: Stand mixer, whisk, or handheld electric mixer

Prep Ahead & Storage Tips

PREP-AHEAD GUIDE

Almost all the recipes in this book can be made ahead in part or completely for easy meal prep throughout the week. We've placed icons at the top of each recipe to indicate how far in advance you can prep a dish before serving and if the dish is freezer friendly!

- **PREP-AHEAD ELEMENT(S)**
  Certain recipe components can be made in advance. See recipe notes for details.
- **PREP UP TO 1 DAY AHEAD**
- **PREP UP TO 2 DAYS AHEAD**
- **PREP UP TO 3 DAYS AHEAD**
- **PREP UP TO 1 WEEK AHEAD**
- **FREEZER-FRIENDLY (UP TO 3 MONTHS)**
  Assemble and freeze or bake first and freeze. See recipe notes for details.

STORAGE TIPS

Use airtight containers to lock in freshness and prevent spills.

Use freezer-safe containers to prevent freezer burn, always leaving space for liquids to expand.

Cool hot foods, including grains and legumes, completely before sealing or storing to prevent condensation and sogginess.

Store liquids such as sauces, salad dressings, and yogurt concoctions separately to keep lettuces crisp and proteins and vegetables from absorbing too much moisture.

Store crisp, fresh, or delicate ingredients separately, including croutons, toasted nuts, seeds, and other salad toppers, to protect their texture.

Label and date containers to track what needs to be eaten first.

Morning Glory

"I love using my Tupperware ice trays for making frozen coffee cubes for my iced coffee so they don't dilute my coffee like regular cubes do—and I use my Ultimate silicone bags to keep my coffee cubes in the freezer."

—GINETTE V.,
8 YEARS SELLING TUPPERWARE PRODUCTS

Ready to give your breakfasts the glow up they deserve? Jump-start the day with a nutrient-rich smoothie (see page 49), tuck into tender and fragrant Ginger Berry Muffins with Cardamom Crumb (page 29), or enjoy a delectable Mini Bagel Egg Ring Sandwich (page 40) with your first cup of coffee—all prepped, stored, and ready when you are. Hosting a breakfast brunch? Serve your guests Coffee Shop–Style Cheddar Bacon Egg Bites (page 39), Dill Crepes with Smoked Trout, Spinach, and Apples (page 43), or Caramelized Apple and Walnut French Toast Bake (page 37) and graciously accept the kudos.

- Simplify batter prep for donuts and pancakes like the Lemon Poppy Seed Donuts with Lemon Glaze (page 25) by mixing everything in the **WHIP 'N MIX CHEF** mixer. You'll end up with a smooth batter you can transfer directly to a ring form or griddle.
- Use the **SIFT 'N STORE** sifter for sifting ingredients or for dusting baked goods with powdered sugar, like the Caramelized Apple and Walnut French Toast Bake (page 37). You can measure and store ingredients in it too.
- When you need melted butter for a recipe, like for the crumb topping on the Ginger Berry Muffins with Cardamom Crumb (page 29), melt it in the microwave using the 1-cup **MICRO PITCHER.**
- Save space in the fridge and mix Overnight Oats (page 22) in an **ULTIMATE SILICONE STAND-UP BAG SMALL.** Mix and refrigerate, then the following morning, pop the reusable silicone bag open, add toppings, and dig in. Stash your toppings in a **SNACK CUP** for adding whenever and wherever your day takes you.

PREP UP TO
3 DAYS AHEAD

MAKES 1 SERVING

Overnight Oats

BASE

¾ cup old-fashioned rolled oats

⅓ cup plain Greek or regular yogurt (dairy or plant based, any fat content)

¾ cup milk (dairy or plant based, any fat content)

2 tablespoons sweetener (such as maple syrup, agave nectar, or honey)

1 teaspoon pure vanilla, almond, or other extract

Pinch of kosher salt

MIX-INS AND/OR TOPPINGS

Fruits and vegetables, such as banana slices, any type of berry, mango cubes, caramelized apples or pears (see page 37), shredded dried coconut, shredded carrot, dried cranberries or raisins, or any type of fruit jam

Nuts and seeds, such as almonds, pecans, walnuts, hemp seeds, or flaxseeds

Nut and fruit butters, such as almond, peanut, cashew, or apple, or canned pumpkin puree

Spices and flavorings, such as ground cardamom, nutmeg, or cinnamon or unsweetened cocoa powder

Endlessly customizable, these nighttime oats are an easy solution to breakfast meal prep: mix and chill, then the following morning, pop the container open, add your topping or toppings of choice, and dig in.

1. In a medium airtight container, combine the oats, yogurt, milk, sweetener, vanilla, salt, and ingredients of your flavor combo of choice. Stir to combine.

2. Securely close the container and place in the refrigerator in an upright position for at least 6 hours or up to overnight before serving.

Mix-In Variations

Cherry Smash: Mix together **½ cup fresh or frozen pitted cherries, chopped;** and **2 tablespoons slivered blanched almonds.**

Pumpkin Pie: Mix together **½ cup canned pumpkin puree, 2 tablespoons pumpkin seeds, 1 tablespoon flaxseeds,** and **¾ teaspoon pumpkin pie spice.**

PB and Choco-Banana: Mix together **2 tablespoons creamy butter** and **1 tablespoon unsweetened cocoa powder.** Top with **1 banana, peeled and sliced.**

Stone Cold Oats: Mix together **1 small, ripe stone fruit (such as apricot, peach, nectarine, or plum), pitted and diced; 1 tablespoon chia seeds;** and **¼ teaspoon ground cinnamon, cardamom, or nutmeg.** Top with more **diced stone fruit.**

PREP UP TO
2 DAYS AHEAD

MAKES 6 DONUTS

Lemon Poppy Seed Donuts with Lemon Glaze

Lemon loaded and glazed, these baked donuts with the nutty crunch of poppy seeds will bring a bright, cheerful vibe to your morning.

DONUTS

¼ cup granulated sugar

Grated zest of 1 lemon, plus 2 tablespoons juice

2 tablespoons vegetable oil

1 teaspoon pure vanilla extract

2 eggs

⅓ cup whole or 2-percent milk

1 tablespoon poppy seeds

1 cup all-purpose flour

1 teaspoon baking powder

½ teaspoon kosher salt

LEMON GLAZE

½ cup powdered sugar

2 tablespoons lemon juice

Grated lemon zest or poppy seeds for garnish

1. Preheat the oven to 350°F. Set a 6-cavity silicone donut form on a metal sheet pan.

2. *Prep the wet mixture:* In a medium bowl, whisk together the sugar and lemon zest. Add the oil and vanilla and whisk until well mixed. Add the eggs, milk, lemon juice, and poppy seeds and whisk until well combined. Set aside.

3. *Prep the dry mixture:* In a separate medium bowl, whisk together the flour, baking powder, and salt. Make a well in the center and pour in the wet mixture. Whisk until no white streaks remain and a smooth batter forms.

4. Fill each cavity three-fourths full with the batter. Bake until the donuts are golden and a toothpick inserted into the center of a donut comes out clean, about 15 minutes. Let cool completely in the donut form on a wire cooling rack before unmolding and glazing.

5. *Meanwhile, make the glaze:* In a small bowl, whisk together the powdered sugar and lemon juice until smooth.

6. Have ready a large serving plate. Dip the top of each donut into the glaze to coat evenly, then set right-side up on the plate. Garnish with lemon zest and let sit for 15 minutes until the glaze has set. Eat now!

Note: Store the donuts in an airtight container at room temperature.

PREP UP TO
3 DAYS AHEAD

SERVES 4

Golden Tofu Scramble

SCRAMBLE

One 14-ounce package extra-firm tofu, drained and patted dry

2 tablespoons nutritional yeast

2 teaspoons ground turmeric

1 teaspoon garlic powder

1 teaspoon onion powder

1 teaspoon kosher salt

2 teaspoons olive oil

1 small red onion, diced

2 small jalapeño chiles or 1 bell pepper (any color), seeded and diced

¼ cup plant-based milk (such as soy or oat)

½ cup plant-based cheese shreds

SERVING SUGGESTIONS

Cooked grains such as quinoa, farro, or couscous

Leafy greens such as baby spinach or arugula

Beans such as black or pinto

Additional vegetables such as cherry tomatoes or corn kernels

Chopped fresh herb such as cilantro or flat-leaf parsley for garnish

Toppings such as hot sauce, salsa, or regular or plant-based chipotle crema (see page 33)

The secret ingredient that takes this scramble from delicious to spectacular is the nutritional yeast (a.k.a. "nooch"), a type of deactivated yeast that's full of B vitamins and has a nutty, cheesy, savory flavor. Seasoned with turmeric, garlic, and onion and splashed with rich plant-based milk, this creamy, bright, and savory tofu scramble is incredibly versatile. Serve it piled on toast, tucked into a pita, or in a wholesome breakfast bowl with vegetables or grains, or use it in place of the egg scramble for a vegan version of Sweet Potato Burritos with Chipotle Crema (page 33).

1. *Make the scramble:* Put the tofu into a medium bowl and mash gently, breaking it up into smaller pieces. Stir in the yeast, turmeric, garlic powder, onion powder, and salt and set aside.

2. In a medium nonstick skillet, heat 1 teaspoon of the oil over medium heat until shimmering. Add the onion and chiles and cook, stirring often, until the chiles start to soften, 2 to 3 minutes.

3. Add the seasoned tofu and milk and cook, stirring often, until the liquid in the pan evaporates, about 1 minute. Add the remaining 1 teaspoon oil and continue to cook until some tofu pieces brown, about 4 minutes. Add the cheese and continue cooking, stirring often, until the cheese melts, about 30 seconds.

4. Serve as you wish!

Note: Store in an airtight container in the fridge. Reheat the scramble in the microwave at 50 percent power for 1 to 2 minutes, stirring halfway through the reheating time. If it's not warmed through, continue reheating in 30-second bursts, stirring between each burst.

PREP UP TO
2 DAYS AHEAD

MAKES 12 MUFFINS

Ginger Berry Muffins with Cardamom Crumb

The secret to these customizable berry-packed muffins is the addition of thick, rich buttermilk to the batter for the fluffiest texture. Ginger scents the muffins themselves, while freshly grated orange zest lifts the fragrance of cardamom in the buttery, crunchy topping.

MUFFINS

¾ cup sugar

Grated zest of 1 small orange, plus 2 tablespoons juice

½ cup vegetable oil

1 teaspoon pure vanilla extract

2 eggs

½ cup whole or 2-percent buttermilk

2 cups all-purpose flour

2 teaspoons baking powder

½ teaspoon ground ginger

½ teaspoon kosher salt

1 cup fresh blueberries, raspberries, blackberries, cranberries, or hulled, sliced strawberries

CRUMB

½ cup all-purpose flour

½ cup sugar

½ teaspoon ground cardamom

½ teaspoon ground nutmeg

¼ teaspoon salt

3 tablespoons unsalted butter, melted

1. Preheat the oven to 375°F. Set two 6-cup silicone muffin forms on a metal sheet pan.

2. *Make the muffins:* In a medium bowl, whisk together the sugar and orange zest. Add the oil and vanilla and whisk until well mixed. Add the eggs, buttermilk, and orange juice and whisk until well combined. Set aside.

3. In a separate medium bowl, whisk together the flour, baking powder, ginger, and salt. Make a well in the center and pour in the egg mixture. Whisk until no white streaks remain and a smooth batter forms. Use a silicone spatula to gently fold the berries into the batter.

4. *Make the crumb topping:* In a small bowl, whisk together the flour, sugar, cardamom, nutmeg, and salt. Pour in the melted butter and stir until crumbs form.

5. Fill each muffin cup three-fourths full with the muffin batter. Top each cup with a heaping tablespoon of the crumb topping, dividing it evenly among the cups. Bake until the tops are golden and a toothpick inserted into the center of a muffin comes out clean, 18 to 20 minutes. Let cool completely in the muffin forms on a wire cooling rack before unmolding.

Note: Store the muffins in an airtight container at room temperature.

PREP AHEAD ELEMENT(S)

PREP UP TO
2 DAYS AHEAD

SERVES 6 TO 8

Banana Date Bread with Sticky Toffee Drizzle

We've elevated classic banana bread into a breakfast treat or brunch knockout with homemade date paste and a decadent sticky toffee drizzle.

DATE PASTE

32 pitted Medjool dates (about 1½ cups)

¾ cup hot water

Pinch of kosher salt

BANANA BREAD

½ cup unsalted butter, at room temperature

⅓ cup granulated sugar

¼ cup packed dark brown sugar

2 eggs, lightly beaten

1½ cups mashed overripe bananas (about 3 medium)

¼ cup plain full-fat yogurt

1¼ teaspoons pure vanilla extract

2 cups all-purpose flour

2 teaspoons baking powder

¾ teaspoon kosher salt

TOFFEE DRIZZLE

4 tablespoons unsalted butter, cut into small pieces

½ cup packed dark brown sugar

½ cup heavy cream

¼ teaspoon pure vanilla extract

Pinch of kosher salt

1. Preheat the oven to 350°F. Butter the bottom and sides of a 9 by 5-inch loaf pan, then dust lightly with flour, tapping out the excess.

2. *Make the date paste:* In a small bowl, combine the dates and hot water and let soak until the dates are soft, about 10 minutes. Drain the dates into a strainer placed over a second small bowl. In a blender, combine the dates, 2 tablespoons of the soaking water, and the salt and blend on medium speed until mostly smooth. Some texture is OK! Set aside.

3. *Make the banana bread:* In a medium bowl, using a handheld mixer, beat together the butter and both sugars on low speed for 30 seconds. Increase the speed to medium and beat until smooth and fluffy, about 3 minutes. Whisk in the eggs until incorporated. Whisk in the bananas, date paste, yogurt, and vanilla until well mixed and smooth.

4. In a separate medium bowl, whisk together the flour, baking powder, and salt. Using a silicone spatula, fold the flour mixture into the banana mixture in three additions until no white streaks remain.

5. Transfer the batter to the prepared loaf pan and smooth the top. Bake until a toothpick inserted into the center comes out clean, about 1 hour. Let cool in the pan on a wire cooling rack for 10 minutes, then unmold onto the rack and let cool completely.

6. *When the banana bread is fully cooled, make the toffee drizzle:* In a medium saucepan, melt the butter over medium heat. Add the sugar and whisk until dissolved. Slowly pour in the cream while whisking

Continued

Banana Date Bread with Sticky Toffee Drizzle, continued

continuously to mix well. Bring the mixture to a gentle boil, lower the heat to a simmer, and cook, whisking constantly, until the mixture thickens, 2 to 3 minutes. Remove from the heat and stir in the vanilla and salt.

7. Place the cooled banana bread on a serving plate. Let the toffee drizzle cool slightly, then drizzle ¼ cup or more evenly over the top of the bread, allowing it to drip down the sides. Slice and serve.

Notes: Store the banana bread in an airtight container at room temperature.

Make the date paste up to 1 week ahead. Store in an airtight container in the fridge. Bring to room temperature before using.

Make the sticky toffee drizzle up to 2 days ahead. Store in an airtight container in the fridge. Warm in the microwave for 20 seconds before using. Use any leftovers on ice cream!

PREP-AHEAD ELEMENT(S)

FREEZER-FRIENDLY UP TO 3 MONTHS

MAKES 6 BURRITOS

Sweet Potato Burritos with Chipotle Crema

These hearty burritos, which are filled with a mix of sweet potatoes, pepper-onion hash, and scrambled eggs and topped with a smoky chipotle crema that ties everything together, are guaranteed to fuel your day. Enjoy them fresh or prep them and freeze them for a grab-and-go meal for self-care wrapped in a tortilla. Want to make them vegan? Omit the onions and peppers in the sweet potato mixture, and once the sweet potatoes are cooked and softened, mix in a ½ recipe Golden Tofu Scramble (page 26).

CHIPOTLE CREMA

1 cup full-fat dairy or plant-based sour cream

1 to 2 tablespoons sauce from canned chipotle chiles in adobo sauce

1 teaspoon garlic powder

¼ teaspoon kosher salt

Grated zest and juice of 2 small limes

FILLING

2 tablespoons olive oil

1 small red onion, diced

2 small jalapeño chiles or 1 bell pepper (any color), seeded and diced

2 medium sweet potatoes, peeled and diced (about 2 cups)

2 teaspoons kosher salt

1 teaspoon smoked paprika

1 teaspoon garlic powder

¼ teaspoon freshly ground black pepper

6 eggs

½ cup shredded cheese (such as sharp Cheddar or Monterey Jack)

BURRITOS

Six 10-inch flour tortillas

4 tablespoons unsalted butter

1. *Make the crema:* In a medium bowl, combine the sour cream, 1 tablespoon of the adobo sauce, the garlic powder, salt, and lime zest and juice and stir to mix well. Taste and adjust with more adobo sauce as desired. Cover and refrigerate until ready to serve.

2. *Make the filling:* In a medium nonstick skillet, heat the oil over medium heat until shimmering. Add the onion and chiles and cook, stirring often, until the chiles start to soften, 2 to 3 minutes.

3. Add the sweet potatoes in a single layer and season with 1 teaspoon of the salt, the paprika, garlic powder, and black pepper. Cook, stirring often, until the potatoes are tender, 7 to 8 minutes. Remove from the heat.

4. In a medium bowl, lightly beat together the eggs and the remaining 1 teaspoon salt. Move the potato mixture to one side of the skillet and return the skillet to medium-low heat. Add the eggs to the empty half of the pan and scramble until just set, about 3 minutes. Gently incorporate the potatoes and continue cooking, stirring often, until the eggs are cooked, about 1 minute more. Fold in the cheese until melted, about 30 seconds more. Remove from the heat.

5. *Fill the burritos:* Scoop about ½ cup of the potato mixture onto a tortilla, placing it just below the center and leave a 1-inch border at the bottom and the sides. Fold the left and right sides over the filling, then bring the bottom up and

Continued

Sweet Potato Burritos with Chipotle Crema, continued

over the filling, tucking it under the edge, and gently roll into a tight burrito. Set aside seam-side down and fill and roll the remaining burritos.

6. Have ready a serving platter. In a large skillet, melt the butter over medium heat. Working in batches if needed to avoid crowding, place the burritos seam-side down in the pan and toast until the underside is golden, about 1 minute. Flip the burritos and toast on the second side until golden, about 30 seconds more. Transfer to the serving platter and serve right away with the crema.

Notes: Store the burritos in an airtight container in the freezer for up to 3 months. Reheat in the microwave at 50 percent power until warmed through, 3 to 4 minutes, flipping them halfway through the reheating time.

Make the crema up to 2 days ahead. Store in an airtight container in the fridge. Stir in a bit more adobo sauce or lime juice to thin as desired before serving.

Tupperware

PREP UP TO
1 DAY AHEAD

SERVES 4 TO 6

Caramelized Apple and Walnut French Toast Bake

The aroma of this French toast bake gives sweater-weather vibes. Better yet, making this irresistible dish is a breeze: while the bread soaks up a silky pumpkin-spiced custard, you can prep the caramelized apple topping. Bonus: the topping doubles as a prep-ahead treat for Overnight Oats (page 22) or for spooning over yogurt.

FRENCH TOAST

- 2 tablespoons unsalted butter, melted
- 1 pound day-old brioche, challah, or sourdough bread, cut into 1-inch cubes
- 6 eggs, at room temperature (see Notes)
- ½ cup plain full-fat Greek yogurt
- 1¾ cups whole or 2-percent milk
- 1 teaspoon pure vanilla extract
- 1½ teaspoons pumpkin pie spice
- 1 teaspoon kosher salt
- ¼ cup packed light brown sugar

APPLE-NUT TOPPING

- 3 medium Honeycrisp or other sweet-tart apples, peeled and cut into ¼-inch-thick slices
- ¼ cup packed dark brown sugar
- 1 teaspoon ground cinnamon
- Pinch of kosher salt
- 1 teaspoon fresh lemon juice
- 2 tablespoons unsalted butter, cut into pieces
- ½ cup finely chopped walnuts

Maple syrup, whipped cream, or powdered sugar for serving

1. Preheat the oven to 375°F.

2. *Make the French toast:* Brush a 9 by 13-inch baking dish with the butter. Add the bread cubes and set aside.

3. In a large bowl, whisk together the eggs, yogurt, milk, vanilla, pie spice, and salt, mixing well. Gently whisk in the brown sugar until dissolved. Pour the mixture over the bread and, using a silicone spatula, toss the bread to coat evenly. Spread the bread in an even layer and set aside to soak in the custard while you prepare the apples.

4. *Make the topping:* In a large bowl, combine the apples, sugar, cinnamon, salt, and lemon juice. Stir to coat the apples evenly.

5. In a large nonstick skillet, melt the butter over medium heat. Add the apples and cook, stirring now and then, until they soften and the juices in the pan thicken and coat the apples in gooey goodness, about 15 minutes. Stir in the walnuts. Remove from the heat.

6. Spread the apple-walnut mixture evenly over the bread in the baking dish and cover the dish. Bake until the custard sets, 20 to 22 minutes. Uncover the dish and continue baking until the top is puffed, the edges of the apple slices are browned, and the nuts are toasted, 8 to 10 minutes more. Remove from the oven.

7. *To serve:* Let cool for 15 minutes, then cut into rectangles and transfer to individual plates. Top each serving with a drizzle of maple syrup, a plop of whipped cream, or a dusting of powdered sugar.

Notes: Room-temperature eggs blend seamlessly with milk, preventing the custard from curdling.

Store the French toast in an airtight container in the fridge. Reheat, covered, in the oven at 350°F until warmed through, 20 to 25 minutes.

PREP UP TO
3 DAYS AHEAD

FREEZER-FRIENDLY
UP TO 3 MONTHS

MAKES 6 EGG BITES

Coffee Shop–Style Cheddar Bacon Egg Bites

6 eggs, or 1¼ cups liquid egg substitute

¾ cup full-fat cottage cheese

¾ cup shredded Cheddar cheese, plus ¼ cup

1 tablespoon cornstarch

¼ teaspoon kosher salt

¼ teaspoon freshly ground black pepper

2 teaspoons apple cider vinegar

6 slices bacon, cooked and finely chopped

2 cups water

This recipe nails the taste and texture of those protein-packed egg bites you love minus the coffee-shop markup. The best part about this recipe is that it's super adaptable!

1. Preheat the oven to 325°F. Place a 6-cup silicone muffin form in a 9 by 13-inch baking dish.

2. In a blender, combine the eggs, cottage cheese, ¾ cup cheese, cornstarch, salt, pepper, and vinegar and blend on high speed until smooth, about 20 seconds.

3. Pour the mixture into the muffin cups, dividing it evenly and filling them to the rim. Scatter the bacon and remaining ¼ cup cheese evenly over the filled cups. Pour the water around the form to create a water bath. This helps the eggs cook evenly.

4. Bake until the tops are golden and the bacon is crispy, about 30 minutes. Remove from the oven and let cool for 10 minutes. Gently unmold by running the tip of a teaspoon around the edges to loosen—it works like a charm! Serve now.

Note: Store the egg bites in an airtight container in the fridge. Reheat in the microwave at 50 percent power until warmed through, about 30 seconds. Why not freeze egg bites for a grab 'n' go brekkie? Reheat frozen egg bites in the microwave at 50 percent power until warmed through, about 1½ minutes.

Variations

Veggie and Cheese: Omit the bacon. Divide **½ cup finely chopped cooked broccoli, spinach, kale, bell peppers, or a combination** evenly among the muffin cups before pouring in the egg mixture and baking.

Fontina and Sausage: Omit the bacon. Swap the Cheddar for fontina cheese. Divide **½ cup crumbled cooked sausage** evenly among the muffin cups before pouring in the egg mixture and baking.

Herb and Cheese: Omit the bacon. Use any good shredding **cheese, such as Cheddar, Gruyère, Monterey Jack, or fontina.** Divide **½ cup chopped fresh herb,** such as basil, evenly among the muffin cups before pouring in the egg mixture and baking.

PREP UP TO
1 DAY AHEAD

FREEZER-FRIENDLY
UP TO 3 MONTHS

MAKES 6 SANDWICHES

Mini Bagel Egg Ring Sandwiches

Egg rings on mini bagels are a small but mighty—and versatile—breakfast sandwich. Create egg rings with your favorite vegetables, herbs, and cheese.

EGG RINGS

3 eggs

⅓ cup whole or 2-percent milk

Pinch of kosher salt

½ cup finely chopped vegetable (such as red onion, bell pepper, or broccoli)

1 tablespoon finely chopped fresh herbs, such as flat-leaf parsley, chives, dill, or basil

SANDWICHES

6 mini bagels, any type, sliced and toasted

6 slices cheese (such as sharp Cheddar or Monterey Jack)

6 breakfast sausage patties (each 2 to 3 inches in diameter) or bacon slices, regular or plant based, cooked

Topping of choice (such as hot sauce, maple syrup, ketchup, or chipotle crema, see page 33)

1. Preheat the oven to 400°F. Set a 6-cavity **SILICONE RING FORM** on a metal sheet pan. Alternatively, use a 6-cavity donut baking pan.

2. *Make the egg rings:* In a medium bowl, whisk together the eggs, milk, and salt until well mixed. Add the vegetables and herbs mix-in and whisk in with a couple of strokes.

3. Fill the molds with the egg mixture, distributing it evenly. Each one should be about three-fourths full.

4. Bake until the eggs are set, about 10 minutes. Remove from the oven and let rest for 5 minutes before unmolding.

5. *Build the sandwiches:* Line up six bagel halves, cut-side up. Place a warm egg ring on each half. Top each egg ring with a cheese slice, folding it as needed so it fits snugly. Set a sausage patty or bacon slice on each cheese slice. If using bacon, fold as needed to fit. Drizzle with your topping of choice, then close the sandwiches with the remaining bagel halves. Enjoy!

Note: Store the sandwiches in an airtight container in the fridge. Reheat the sandwiches in the microwave at 50 percent power until warmed through, about 30 seconds. Or store the sandwiches in an airtight container in the freezer. Reheat frozen sandwiches in the microwave at 50 percent power until warmed through, about 1½ minutes.

PREP-AHEAD ELEMENT(S)

MAKES 8 9-INCH CREPES

Dill Crepes with Smoked Trout, Spinach, and Apples

SMOKED TROUT FILLING

3 tablespoons cream cheese, at room temperature

2 tablespoons plain full-fat Greek yogurt

2 tablespoons finely chopped fresh dill

1 small shallot, finely chopped

Grated zest of 1 lemon

½ teaspoon kosher salt

Two 3.9-ounce cans smoked trout fillets in oil, drained and flaked

CREPES

1 tablespoon finely chopped fresh dill

1¼ cups whole or 2-percent milk, at room temperature

½ teaspoon kosher salt

1 cup all-purpose flour, sifted

2 eggs, at room temperature

1 tablespoon unsalted butter, melted and cooled, plus 2 tablespoons, cut into small pieces

1 teaspoon vegetable oil, plus more as needed

Small bunch fresh spinach leaves (about 1 cup packed), tough stems trimmed

1 green apple, julienned (see Notes, page 44)

Chopped fresh dill for garnish

Lemon wedges for serving

These soft, savory dill crepes are everything you want in an entertainment-worthy brunch dish: they are flavorful, simple to make, and look elegant when plated. The filling of rich smoked trout and crisp spinach leaves is nicely balanced by a garnish of julienned tart green apple.

1. Line two metal sheet pans with silicone baking sheets. Set out a serving platter.

2. *Make the smoked trout filling:* In a medium bowl, combine the cream cheese, yogurt, dill, shallot, lemon zest, and salt. Using a silicone spatula, mix together until smooth. Add the trout and mix until well distributed but the mixture still has texture.

3. *Make the crepe batter:* In a blender, combine the dill, milk, salt, flour, eggs, and melted butter and blend on medium speed until smooth. If time allows, let the mixture sit for 30 minutes. This short "rest" yields a more tender crepe.

4. *Cook the crepes:* In a 9-inch nonstick skillet, warm the oil over medium heat until shimmering, tilting the pan to coat the bottom evenly (see Notes, page 44). Pour ¼ cup of the batter into the center of the pan, then tilt and swirl the skillet to spread the batter evenly. Cook undisturbed until the surface looks dry and the edges lift easily, 1 to 2 minutes. Gently slide a silicone spatula under the edge of the crepe, then use your fingers to lift and flip the crepe. Cook the second side until it releases from the pan, about 15 seconds, and then slide it onto a prepared sheet pan. Repeat with the remaining batter, adding more oil to the pan if needed. Once cooked, arrange the crepes on the two prepared sheet pans so they don't stick to one another. You should have eight crepes in all.

5. *Fill the crepes:* Working with one crepe at a time, spread about 2 tablespoons of the trout filling across the top,

Continued

Dill Crepes with Smoked Trout, Spinach, and Apples, continued

leaving a ½-inch border. Top the filling with two or three spinach leaves. Fold the crepe in half to cover the filling, creating a half-moon. Fold the crepe in half again to create a triangle with two layers. Repeat with the remaining crepes and filling.

6. In the now-empty skillet, melt half of the butter pieces over medium-low heat. Add a filled crepe and toast, turning once, until golden on both sides, about 30 seconds on each side. Transfer to the serving platter. Repeat with the remaining crepes, adding more butter to the pan as needed and arranging the crepes on the serving platter as you work.

7. Garnish the crepes with the apple and dill. Serve right away, with lemon wedges for squeezing over the top.

Notes: To prevent the cut apples from turning brown, squeeze a lemon wedge over them.

You can use an 8-inch, 9-inch, or 10-inch nonstick skillet or crepe pan. The larger your pan, the thinner your crepe.

Make the trout filling up to 3 days ahead. Store in an airtight container in the fridge. Let it sit out for 20 to 30 minutes to soften, then give it a stir before using. It also doubles as a great party dip with crackers!

MAKES 1 OMELET

Fine Herb and Feta Omelet

2 eggs

1 tablespoon whole or 2-percent milk or water

1 tablespoon finely chopped mixed fresh soft herbs (such as flat-leaf parsley and dill)

¼ cup crumbled feta cheese

Toast, any type, for serving

This recipe uses a handy Tupperware product—the **MICROWAVE BREAKFAST MAKER**—to make a delicious, flavorful omelet quickly and easily. It is the perfect morning meal for busy bees, college kids, solo eaters, and short-order cooks (ahem, parents). Plus, no "skill"-et required.

1. In a small bowl, whisk together the eggs, milk, and herbs, mixing well. Stir in the feta cheese.

2. Transfer the egg mixture to the **MICROWAVE BREAKFAST MAKER**. Cover with the lid and microwave at 50 percent power until the eggs are set, 3 to 4 minutes. Let rest for 1 minute, then slide onto a plate. Serve immediately with toast.

Variation

To make it your own, add **¼ cup each of finely chopped cooked vegetables (any type), cooked and diced breakfast meat,** and/or shredded or crumbled **cheese of choice.**

FREEZER-FRIENDLY
UP TO 3 MONTHS

MAKES 1 SMOOTHIE

Jump-Start Smoothie Packs

Watermelon Cucumber Coconut Smoothie

SMOOTHIE PACK

1 cup diced watermelon

½ cup diced English or Persian cucumber

2 tablespoons fresh lime juice

3 fresh mint leaves

BLEND

1 cup coconut water

1 teaspoon honey (see Note)

Chocolate Date Smoothie

SMOOTHIE PACK

1½ cups chopped banana

6 dates, pitted and chopped

BLEND

1 cup milk

2 tablespoons nut butter

1 to 2 tablespoons unsweetened cocoa powder

Banana Chai Smoothie

SMOOTHIE PACK

1 cup chopped banana

½ cup sliced peach

½-inch piece fresh ginger, peeled and sliced

BLEND

1 cup milk

1 teaspoon chai tea spice blend

1 teaspoon honey (see Note)

Creamy Green Protein Smoothie

SMOOTHIE PACK

1 cup packed baby spinach leaves

½ cup diced pineapple

¼ cup banana slices

¼ cup riced cauliflower

BLEND

1 cup milk

2 tablespoons vanilla protein powder

1 teaspoon honey (see Note)

1. *Prep the smoothie pack:* Put the smoothie pack ingredients into a small silicone bag and freeze.

2. When ready to serve, allow the smoothie pack to thaw on the counter, about 10 minutes.

3. *Blend the smoothie:* Add the thawed contents of the pack to blender. Add the blend ingredients and blend on high speed until completely smooth. Pour into a glass and serve.

Note: You can swap out the honey for maple syrup or agave nectar.

Sensational Salads

"I've learned that it is okay to make mistakes—everyone is human—and find the humor in it and connect with people through the 'oops.'"

—LARISSA V.,
4 YEARS SELLING TUPPERWARE PRODUCTS

In this chapter, fresh, vibrant salads with signature textures, flavorful add-ins, and luscious dressings bring the perfect balance of ease and excitement to meals!

With just a little planning and creativity, salads can pop with possibilities. Imagine this: You open your fridge to find not a mess of leftovers forgotten in random containers but rather a rainbow of already-prepped salad ingredients and add-ins, stacked and organized, ready to inspire your next creation. (We promise it's possible! See page 53.) In this chapter, we'll guide you through making salads for effortless weeknight dinners, tasty lunches, and showstopping party favorites.

- Prep and keep "from scratch" salad dressings in the **ALL-IN-ONE SHAKER.**
- **SALAD ON THE GO SET** is a delightful and practical container for bringing a sensational salad to work or school. For convenience, the utensils and the dressing container attach to the leakproof lid!
- The **PICK-A-DELI** container is a pickle hero! With its liftable strainer, it keeps your fingers dry while storing Any Quick Pickle (page 79), olives, tofu, and mozzarella in their liquid. And it's great for making Pink Pickled Eggs (page 206).
- Keep your produce crisp and ready for action with the **FRIDGESMART** containers. Their unique venting system helps extend the life of your fresh greens, herbs, and veggies.
- Up your in-fridge salad bar with **ONE TOUCH FRESH** containers. Their airtight, press-to-seal lids lock in freshness while the see-through design lets you quickly spot your prepped ingredients.

PREP-AHEAD ELEMENT(S)

SERVES 4

Dilly Chopped Salad with Pickle Ranch Dressing

SALAD

1 English or 2 Persian cucumbers, halved lengthwise, seeded, and cut crosswise into half-moons

1 teaspoon kosher salt

2 romaine lettuce hearts, core trimmed and leaves cut into bite-size pieces

3 celery stalks with tender leaves, thinly sliced

½ cup minced red onion (from ½ small onion)

12 cherry tomatoes, halved

2 cups Garlic Croutons (page 78)

2 tablespoons finely chopped fresh dill, plus fronds for garnish

DILL PICKLE RANCH DRESSING

½ cup mayonnaise

¼ cup whole or 2-percent buttermilk, plus more if needed

¼ cup full-fat sour cream

½ cup finely chopped dill pickles or cucumber quick pickles (see page 79), plus 2 tablespoons pickle brine

1 tablespoon dried dill

1 garlic clove, minced

½ teaspoon kosher salt

¼ teaspoon freshly ground black pepper

This salad was made for all the pickle fans in your life. We promise that if you have an adventurous pickle lovin' kid, the dressing will be a major hit. It's creamy and zingy, and it also doubles as a dipping sauce for fries, chicken tenders, and raw veggies. Enjoy this crunchy salad as is or toss in a hearty protein, such as Crispy Tofu Strips (page 128), black or pinto beans, or chopped or shredded cooked chicken (see page 112). Dreaming of that protein but short on time? Grab a rotisserie chicken from the store, remove the skin and bones, and shred the meat into bite-size pieces.

1. *Prep the cucumber:* Put the cucumber slices into a colander, sprinkle with the salt, and toss well. Let sit for 15 minutes. The salt will draw out the water from the slices and firm them up, making them extra crunchy. Pat the cucumber slices dry with a clean kitchen towel.

2. *Meanwhile, make the dressing:* In a small bowl, whisk together the mayonnaise, buttermilk, sour cream, pickles and pickle brine, dill, garlic, salt, and pepper until smooth. Whisk in more buttermilk, 1 tablespoon at a time, as needed to achieve a good consistency. Taste and adjust with salt and pepper if needed.

3. *Assemble the salad:* In a large bowl, combine the cucumber slices, lettuce, celery, onion, tomatoes, croutons, and chopped dill. Drizzle with the dressing and toss to coat evenly. Get fancy and garnish with the dill fronds. Serve and crunch!

Notes: Assemble the salad up to 1 day ahead, omitting the croutons and dressing. Store covered in the fridge. Add the croutons and dressing just before serving.

Make the dressing up to 2 days ahead. Store in an airtight container in the fridge.

Make the croutons up to 1 week ahead. Store in an airtight container at room temperature.

PREP-AHEAD ELEMENT(S)

SERVES 4 TO 6

Antipasto Affair

This salad brings the "little of this and little of that" feel-good vibes of a classic antipasto platter—salty, porky punches of cured meat, sharp provolone, briny green olives, and tart-sweet-tangy sun-dried tomatoes. It's also a stellar "clean out the fridge" salad to use up the odds and ends of your favorite cured meats and cheeses. Grilled zucchini spears bring earthy sweetness, a pop of color, and balance. Little Gem lettuce is a petite butter and romaine hybrid, but if you can't find Little Gem, you can use romaine lettuce instead.

ITALIAN VINAIGRETTE

⅓ cup extra-virgin olive oil

3 tablespoons red wine vinegar

2 teaspoons Dijon mustard

2 tablespoons finely chopped fresh oregano

¼ teaspoon kosher salt

Pinch of freshly ground pepper

ZUCCHINI

2 medium zucchini, ends trimmed, quartered lengthwise into spears

2 tablespoons extra-virgin olive oil

½ teaspoon kosher salt

Pinch of freshly ground pepper

SALAD

3 Little Gem lettuce heads

1 medium red onion, thinly sliced

One 6-ounce length spicy or sweet salami, halved lengthwise and cut crosswise into ⅛-inch-thick half-moons

4 ounces sliced cooked ham or prosciutto, cut into narrow strips

1 cup cubed sharp provolone

½ cup oil-packed sun-dried tomatoes, drained and sliced

6 canned artichoke hearts, drained and halved

6 to 8 peperoncini, drained

20 pitted Castelvetrano olives

2 cups Garlic Croutons (page 78)

6 fresh basil leaves, torn

6 Black Pepper Parmigiano-Reggiano Crisps (page 79), optional

1. *Make the vinaigrette:* In medium bowl, whisk together the oil, vinegar, mustard, oregano, salt, and pepper until the oil and vinegar come together. Set aside.

2. *Prep the zucchini:* Prepare a grill for direct cooking over high heat or preheat a stovetop grill pan over high heat. Set a large plate near the grill or stovetop. Brush the zucchini spears with the oil, then season with the salt and pepper. Place the zucchini spears on the grill grates or grill pan and cook undisturbed until they soften and there are grill marks on the underside, about 6 minutes. Flip the spears and cook until the second side is tender, about 4 minutes more. Transfer to a plate and let cool.

3. *Assemble the salad:* Separate the leaves and discard the core of the lettuce heads. Pour half of the dressing into a medium bowl. Add the lettuce and onion and toss to coat evenly. Add the salami, ham, provolone, sun-dried tomatoes, artichoke hearts, peperoncini, olives, croutons, and basil and toss once more, adding more dressing as needed to coat lightly but evenly. Arrange the salad on a large serving platter with the zucchini alongside. Top with the crisps, if using, and serve now!

Notes: Make the vinaigrette up to 2 days ahead. Store in an airtight container in the fridge.

Make the zucchini up to 2 days ahead. Store in an airtight container in the fridge.

Make the croutons up to 1 week ahead. Store in an airtight container at room temperature.

PREP-AHEAD ELEMENT(S)

SERVES 4

Peachy Green with Goat Cheese and Nut Clusters

MAPLE BALSAMIC VINAIGRETTE

⅓ cup extra-virgin olive oil

2 tablespoons balsamic vinegar

1½ tablespoons maple syrup

1½ teaspoons Dijon mustard

1 small shallot, minced

½ teaspoon kosher salt

¼ teaspoon freshly ground black pepper

WHIPPED GOAT CHEESE

One 10-ounce log fresh goat cheese, at room temperature

2 tablespoons extra-virgin olive oil

1 tablespoon honey, plus more if needed

¼ teaspoon kosher salt

PEACHES

2 barely ripe freestone peaches, halved, pitted, and cut into ¼-inch-thick slices

1 tablespoon extra-virgin olive oil

1 teaspoon honey

1 tablespoon finely chopped fresh rosemary

Pinch of kosher salt

SALAD

6 cups packed mixed young salad greens or spring mix (such as red and green lettuces, arugula, endive, frisée, and mustard greens)

1 cup Sweet or Spicy Maple Nut Clusters (page 78)

Elevate an everyday green salad by adding honey-kissed whipped goat cheese, sweet grilled peaches or pears, and crunchy maple nut morsels. The maple balsamic dressing adds complementary caramel and tang. Not in the mood for salad? Skip the fruit, greens, and nut clusters and enjoy the whipped goat cheese as a dip for fresh fruit, crackers, or veggies, topping it with a drizzle of extra-virgin olive oil and your favorite snipped fresh herbs just before serving. Let the goat cheese often on the counter before you begin whipping them together. When peaches are out of season, use 2 Comice, Bartlett, or other sweet, firm pears, cored and sliced, in their place.

1. *Make the vinaigrette:* In a small bowl, whisk together the oil, vinegar, maple syrup, mustard, shallot, salt, and pepper until the oil and vinegar come together. Set aside.

2. *Prep the whipped goat cheese:* In a medium bowl, combine the goat cheese, oil, honey, and salt. Using a handheld mixer, whip together on medium speed until smooth and creamy, stopping to scrape down the sides of the bowl as necessary. Taste and add more honey for sweetness, if desired.

3. *Prep the peaches:* Prepare a grill for direct cooking over high heat or preheat a stovetop grill pan over high heat. While the grill or pan heats, in a medium bowl, toss together the peaches, oil, honey, rosemary, and salt until the peach slices are well coated.

4. Set a plate near the grill or stovetop. Arrange the peach slices flesh-side down on the grill grates or grill pan and grill undisturbed until they soften and there are grill marks on the underside, about 10 minutes. Flip the slices and cook until the second side is softened and juicy at the edges, about 2 minutes more. Transfer to the plate and let cool for 10 to 15 minutes.

5. *Assemble the salad:* Have ready four individual serving plates. Spread about one-fourth of the whipped goat cheese across the bottom

Continued

Peachy Green with Goat Cheese and Nut Clusters, continued

of each plate. It will anchor the greens and ensure you get a bit of cheese in each bite. In a large bowl, combine the greens, peaches, and nut clusters. Drizzle with the dressing and toss to coat evenly. Divide evenly among the plates and serve right away.

Notes: Make the dressing up to 2 days ahead. Store in an airtight container in the fridge.

Prep the peaches up to 1 day ahead. Store in an airtight container in the fridge.

Prep the whipped goat cheese up to 3 days ahead. Store in an airtight container in the fridge. Let it sit out for 20 minutes to soften before using.

PREP-AHEAD ELEMENT(S)

SERVES 6

Kale Shrimp Caesar

SHRIMP

1 pound large tail-on shrimp, peeled and deveined (16 to 20 shrimp)

1 garlic clove, minced

Grated zest of 1 lemon, plus 1 tablespoon juice

2 tablespoons extra-virgin olive oil

¼ teaspoon kosher salt

Pinch of freshly ground black pepper

PANKO CRUMBS

1 tablespoon extra-virgin olive oil

½ cup panko bread crumbs

¼ teaspoon kosher salt

Pinch of freshly ground black pepper

½ teaspoon garlic powder

This version of a Caesar salad beats a premade salad kit any day, and the homemade dressing is a cinch to make. Kale, rather than romaine, will give you a sturdy base for the dressing to cling to, and toasty panko crumbs offer feathery, light texture throughout. (For classic crunch, add Garlic Croutons, page 78.) Enjoy with shrimp hot off the grill or prep them ahead and chill. You can also swap in shredded cooked chicken (see page 112), or skip the protein and dig into the dressed kale, showered in cheese.

1. *Marinate the shrimp:* In a medium bowl, combine the shrimp, garlic, lemon zest and juice, olive oil, salt, and pepper and toss to coat the shrimp evenly. Cover and refrigerate for 30 minutes. Meanwhile, prep the other stuff.

2. *Prep the panko crumbs:* In a large skillet, warm the olive oil over medium heat. Add the panko in an even layer and, using a wooden spoon or heat-resistant silicone spatula, stir continuously until golden brown and toasty, 3 to 4 minutes. Stir in the salt, pepper, and garlic powder. Remove from the heat and set aside.

3. *Make the Caesar dressing:* In a blender, combine the egg yolks, lemon juice, mustard, garlic, anchovy fillets, Worcestershire sauce, salt, and pepper and blend on medium speed until smooth. With the blender running on low speed, slowly stream in the canola oil and olive oil, blending until the dressing is thick and creamy. Transfer to a small bowl and stir in the cheese. Taste and add more salt if needed. Cover and refrigerate until ready to use.

4. *Grill the shrimp:* Prepare a grill for direct cooking over high heat or preheat a stovetop grill pan over high heat. Set a large plate near the grill or stovetop. Arrange the shrimp in a single layer on the grill grates or grill pan and grill, turning once, until bright pink and opaque, 1 to 2 minutes on each side. Transfer to the plate.

5. *Assemble the salad:* Pour the dressing into a large bowl. Add the kale and lemon juice and toss until the kale is thoroughly coated. Add the grilled shrimp,

Continued

Kale Shrimp Caesar, continued

CAESAR DRESSING

2 egg yolks (see Notes)

2 tablespoons fresh lemon juice

1 tablespoon Dijon mustard

1 garlic clove, minced

4 anchovy fillets packed in olive oil

2 teaspoons Worcestershire sauce

¼ teaspoon kosher salt

Pinch of freshly ground black pepper

¼ cup canola or other neutral vegetable oil

¼ cup extra-virgin olive oil

¼ cup grated Parmigiano-Reggiano cheese

SALAD

8 cups packed curly kale, tough stems removed, sliced into ribbons (from about 1 bunch or 5 ounces)

2 tablespoons fresh lemon juice

1 cup halved cherry tomatoes

3-ounce wedge Parmigiano-Reggiano or grana padano cheese

tomatoes, and toasted panko and toss once more. Divide the salad among individual plates and, using a mini grater, shower each serving with cheese. Dig in!

Notes: Consuming raw egg yolks can pose a risk to pregnant or older persons, young children, and people with compromised immune systems. Save the egg whites from the dressing for making Chocolate-Dipped Coconut Macaroons (page 194).

Grill the shrimp up to 2 days ahead. Store in an airtight container in the fridge. Serve cold when assembling the salad.

Make the Caesar dressing up to 2 days ahead. Store in an airtight container in the fridge.

PREP UP TO
1 DAY AHEAD

SERVES 4 TO 6

Layered Greek Salad

Here is the answer the next time you're wondering, "What can I bring?" Think Greek and roll up to any gathering with this beautifully layered salad. Pro tip: serve the salad in a clear bowl; the vibrant layers of fresh greens, crispy cucumbers, minty rice, and colorful onions, tomatoes, and bell peppers will make this a hit with guests. When you're ready to serve, the tzatziki dressing layer pulls all the components together. Look for marinated feta rather than a plain block. The herbs, oils, and spices in the marinade will flavor the cheese—and the salad.

TZATZIKI DRESSING

1 English cucumber

2 teaspoons kosher salt

2 garlic cloves, minced

2 tablespoons extra-virgin olive oil, plus more if needed

1½ cups plain full-fat Greek yogurt

¼ cup full-fat sour cream

¼ cup finely chopped fresh mint leaves

Juice of ½ lemon

SALAD

2 cups cooked, cooled long-grain rice (such as jasmine)

1 teaspoon kosher salt

¼ cup finely chopped fresh mint leaves

1 romaine lettuce heart, core trimmed and leaves chopped into bite-size pieces

2 cups baby spinach leaves

1 English or 2 Persian cucumbers, halved lengthwise, seeded, and cut into ½-inch dice

1 small red onion, thinly sliced

2 cups halved cherry tomatoes

1½ cups pitted Kalamata olives

6 ounces marinated, crumbled feta cheese

2 bell peppers (any color or a mixture), seeded and cut into ¼-inch dice

1. *Make the dressing:* Set a fine-mesh strainer over a medium bowl. Finely grate the cucumber into the strainer. Sprinkle with the salt and stir to mix, then let sit for 10 minutes to allow the cucumber to release its water. Then, using a silicone spatula, press the cucumber against the sides of the strainer, releasing the excess water into the bowl.

2. Transfer the drained cucumber to a medium bowl. Add the garlic and oil and stir to mix well. Then add the yogurt, sour cream, mint, and lemon juice and stir until well mixed and smooth. If the dressing is thick, stir in more oil, a teaspoon at a time, for a more spreadable consistency. Cover and refrigerate until ready to use.

3. *Assemble the salad:* Add the rice, salt, and mint to the bottom of a clear (16¾ cup) salad bowl with a lid. Stir to combine, then spread in an even layer. Layer the romaine over the rice, followed by the spinach, filling along the perimeter first so the ingredients are visible from the sides of the bowl. Then layer the cucumber, onion, tomatoes, olives, feta, and bell peppers on top. Spoon the dressing evenly over the layered ingredients and smooth the top. Cover the bowl and refrigerate until ready to serve.

4. *To serve:* Using a long-handled serving spoon, scoop straight down along the edge of the bowl to the bottom, then gently lift and transfer the scoop to a serving plate. The spoon will catch a bit of each layer per portion. Invite guests to mix their portion on their plate.

Notes: Assemble the entire salad, dressing included, up to 1 day ahead. Store covered in the fridge.

Use the tzatziki dressing on a Mediterranean Falafel Patty Platter (page 141) or with Chicken Kofta Slab Kebabs (page 177).

PREP UP TO
3 DAYS AHEAD

SERVES 4 TO 6

Kohlrabi and Brussels Sprouts Crunch

1½ cups walnut halves

2 pounds kohlrabi bulbs (about 4 medium bulbs), leaves trimmed (save for sautéing) and bulbs peeled, cut crosswise into ½-inch-thick rounds, then cubed

4 tablespoons extra-virgin olive oil, plus more if needed

1½ teaspoons kosher salt

½ teaspoon freshly ground black pepper

8 cups shredded brussels sprouts (from about 1½ pounds)

Juice of 1 lemon

½ cup golden raisins

1½ cups grated pecorino romano cheese

This crunchy, lemony, cheese-rich salad of hearty brussels sprouts and tender roasted kohlrabi stays fresh and delicious for up to 3 days in the fridge. It is also deliciously versatile: a satisfying lunch to tote to work, a tasty snack to munch on between work meetings, or a complementary partner for Herb Roasted Chicken (page 200) or Spiced Yogurt Baked Salmon (page 220).

1. *Toast the walnuts and roast the kohlrabi:* Position one rack in the upper third of the oven and one rack in the lower third of oven, then preheat the oven to 400°F.

2. Line a metal sheet pan with a silicone baking sheet. Spread the walnuts in a single layer on the sheet pan.

3. In a medium bowl, toss the kohlrabi cubes with 1 tablespoon of the oil, ½ teaspoon of the salt, and ¼ teaspoon of the pepper, coating evenly. Transfer to a 2-quart casserole pan, spreading in an even layer.

4. Place the sheet pan on the upper rack of the oven and the casserole pan on the lower rack of the oven. Toast the walnuts until they are fragrant and begin to brown, about 7 minutes. Remove the walnuts from the oven, let cool until they can be handled, and then chop and set aside. Continue roasting the kohlrabi, stirring halfway during the cooking time, until tender and golden, about 20 minutes more. Remove from the oven and set aside to cool to room temperature, about 30 minutes.

5. *Assemble the salad:* Add the brussels sprouts to a large bowl. Season with the remaining 1 teaspoon salt and ¼ teaspoon pepper and the lemon juice and toss to combine. Add the kohlrabi, walnuts, raisins, cheese, and the remaining 3 tablespoons oil and toss until the vegetables are well coated, adding more oil if you wish. Enjoy now!

Note: Store in an airtight container in the fridge. The lemon juice will soften the vegetables slightly, giving them a more tender texture.

TUPPERWARE®

PREP-AHEAD ELEMENT(S)

SERVES 4

Summer Tomato, Green Olive, and Halloumi

TOMATOES

2 pounds ripe heirloom tomatoes in a mix of colors, cored, halved, and sliced into ½-inch-thick half-moons

1 small red onion, thinly sliced

4 tablespoons extra-virgin olive oil

2 tablespoons red wine vinegar

5 fresh basil leaves, torn, plus more for garnish

½ teaspoon kosher salt

½ cup Castelvetrano or other green olives, pitted and smashed

1 medium-ripe avocado, halved, pitted, peeled, and thinly sliced

½ medium orange

HALLOUMI

One 8-ounce package halloumi cheese, cut into ½-inch-thick planks

Olive oil for brushing

1 crusty baguette, sliced, for serving

Pairing peak-season tomatoes with warm halloumi cheese, creamy avocado, and smashed briny olives tastes like a summer day. Halloumi, originating from Cyprus, squeaks when you bite it, and when you sear it in a skillet on the stovetop or grill it, the inside stays soft and warm while the exterior develops a golden crust. We marinate the tomatoes and red onion to mellow the sharpness of the onion and to help the tomatoes release their juices.

1. *Prep the tomatoes:* In a large bowl, combine the tomatoes, onion, 2 tablespoons of the oil, the vinegar, basil, and salt. Toss gently to coat evenly. Cover and marinate in the refrigerator for 1 hour for optimum flavor. (You can skip this step if you are pressed for time.)

2. Add the olives and avocado to the tomatoes and toss gently to distribute evenly. Transfer the salad to a serving platter and squeeze the juice from the orange half over the top. Set aside.

3. *Make the halloumi:* Warm a large cast-iron skillet over medium heat. Brush the halloumi planks on both sides with oil and arrange in a single layer in the skillet. Cook undisturbed, flipping once halfway through the cooking time, until golden brown on both sides, 2½ to 2 minutes on each side.

4. Top the salad with the warm halloumi and garnish with more basil. Serve now with the baguette slices for sopping up the dressing.

Note: Prep the tomatoes in the marinade 1 hour in advance of assembling the salad to heighten their flavor.

PREP-AHEAD ELEMENT(S)

SERVES 4

Beet, Bulgur, and Blue Cheese with Orange Vinaigrette

ORANGE VINAIGRETTE

⅓ cup extra-virgin olive oil

2 tablespoons apple cider vinegar

Juice of 1 orange

2 teaspoons Dijon mustard

1 teaspoon honey

1 medium shallot, minced

¼ teaspoon kosher salt

¼ teaspoon freshly ground black pepper

SALAD

½ cup walnut or pecan halves

½ cup medium-coarse grind bulgur

1¼ cups water

4 cups packed arugula or baby spinach leaves (or an equal mix)

1 small red onion, thinly sliced, or red onion quick pickles (see page 79)

2 medium raw beets, ends trimmed, peeled, and julienned (see headnote), or 2 medium cooked beets, julienned

2 medium oranges (such as navel or Cara Cara), peeled, pith removed, and segmented or cut into rounds

¼ teaspoon kosher salt

¼ teaspoon freshly ground black pepper

½ cup crumbled blue cheese

This salad hits so many gratifying notes: hearty bulgur, bursts of fresh orange, toasted nuts, bold blue cheese, and crunchy, earthy, sweet julienned beets. To julienne, or "French cut," means to cut raw veggies or fruits into matchsticks, taking texture up a notch—oh là là! Try it with carrots, cucumbers, zucchini, jicama, apples, and pears. You can also julienne cooked beets if you already have them on hand. To julienne beets by hand, using a sharp knife, first slice the beets crosswise into ¼-inch-thick rounds, then stack a few rounds at a time and cut each stack into ¼-inch-wide strips.

1. *Make the orange vinaigrette:* In medium bowl, whisk together the oil, vinegar, orange juice, mustard, honey, shallot, salt, and pepper until the oil and vinegar come together. Set aside.

2. *Toast the nuts:* In a dry small skillet, toast the nuts over medium heat, tossing constantly, until fragrant and beginning to brown, 3 to 5 minutes. Pour into a small bowl and let cool.

3. *Prep the bulgur:* In a small saucepan, combine the bulgur and water and bring to a boil over high heat. Turn down the heat to medium-low and gently simmer until the water is absorbed, 10 to 12 minutes. Remove the pan from the heat, cover, and let sit for 5 minutes. Uncover and fluff the bulgur with a fork. Set aside to cool for 15 minutes.

4. *Assemble the salad:* In a large bowl, combine the bulgur, arugula, onion, beets, oranges, and walnuts—the bulgur will turn pink! Toss gently to mix. Season with the salt and pepper. Drizzle with the dressing and toss to coat evenly. Sprinkle with the cheese and serve.

Notes: Assemble the salad up to 1 day ahead, omitting the dressing and cheese. Store covered in the fridge. Top with the cheese and add the dressing just before serving.

Make the dressing up to 2 days ahead. Store in an airtight container in the fridge.

PREP-AHEAD ELEMENT(S)

SERVES 4 TO 6

Creamy Tahini Wedge Salad with Roasted Grapes and Feta

This crunchy iceberg wedge smothered in a creamy tahini-laced yogurt-based dressing, peppery radishes, salty feta, and candy-sweet roasted grapes is ideal for a DIY wedge salad bar for a brunch or lunchtime gathering. Just set iceberg wedges on a board or platter and the dressing, grapes, radishes, feta, and sesame seeds in bowls alongside. Then set out additional bowls of new and classic toppings, such as crispy bacon, chopped hard-boiled eggs, chopped fresh chives, blue cheese crumbles, pickled red onions, and avocado slices, and let guests serve themselves.

CREAMY TAHINI DRESSING

1 cup plain full-fat Greek yogurt

¼ cup extra-virgin olive oil

¼ cup tahini

Juice of 1 lemon

1 garlic clove, minced

1 teaspoon ground cumin

½ teaspoon kosher salt

ROASTED GRAPES

2 cups seedless red or green grapes, halved

2 teaspoons olive oil

¼ teaspoon kosher salt

SALAD

2 small heads iceberg lettuce, each cut into 4 wedges

8 radishes, thinly sliced

½ cup crumbled feta cheese

2 tablespoons toasted sesame seeds

1. Preheat the oven to 400°F. Line a metal sheet pan with a silicone baking sheet.

2. *Make the tahini dressing:* In a medium bowl, whisk together the yogurt, oil, tahini, lemon juice, garlic, cumin, and salt until smooth. Slowly whisk in water, 1 tablespoon at a time, to thin the dressing to a good consistency, keeping in mind the water-rich lettuce will dilute it further as you eat. Set aside.

3. *Roast the grapes:* In a medium bowl, toss together the grapes, oil, and salt. Arrange the grapes in a single layer on the prepared sheet pan. Roast until they release their juices and are slightly shriveled, 12 to 15 minutes. Let cool completely before using.

4. *Assemble the salad:* Place the wedges on a family-style serving platter. Drizzle as much dressing as you prefer over the tops and among the layers of leaves. Serve any remaining dressing on the side. Scatter the radishes, grapes, and cheese over the top. Sprinkle the wedges with sesame seeds. Enjoy!

Notes: Make the dressing up to 2 days ahead. Store in an airtight container in the fridge. Stir in a squeeze of fresh lemon juice to loosen the dressing before using.

Make the roasted grapes up to 2 days ahead. Store in an airtight container in the fridge.

In-Fridge Salad Bar

Our In-Fridge Salad Bar is exactly what it sounds like. Wash, chop, and prep your preferred salad items in advance. Label each container and store them all in your fridge for mix-and-match ingredients on demand, simplifying your meal prep, minimizing food waste, and keeping everything fresh, accessible, and organized. Your salad creativity will soar!

A truly delicious, satisfying salad is made of a few key yet impactful elements: fresh produce, bright colors, a sprinkle of sweetness, a punch of crunch, and a dash of something vinegary to bring it all together—and if you want to go big, satisfying grain and/or protein add-ins.

And don't forget the homemade dressings! Toss in some simple prep techniques—massaging kale; quick pickling, roasting, shaving, or spiralizing veggies; toasting nuts and seeds—and you'll be on your way to becoming a salad pro. Use this guide to inform the salad recipes on pages 54 to 83, inspire your salad creations, and raise your salad bar.

LETTUCES AND HERBS

Fresh herbs, when combined with lettuces, add aroma, zing, and complexity to salad greens. Grab them by the handful and use them with generosity in your salad preparations and dressings. Try these combos:

Arugula + Basil or Mint—Peppery bite meets sweet, aromatic freshness.

Baby Spinach + Dill or Flat-Leaf Parsley—Mild green gets a bright, grassy lift.

Bibb Lettuce + Tarragon—Buttery texture takes on a light anise note.

Iceberg Lettuce + Chives or Flat-Leaf Parsley—Crisp and neutral welcomes an oniony or herbal boost.

Kale (Curly or Lacinato) + Basil or Mint—Earthy green gets a fresh lift.

Little Gem Lettuce + Chervil or Tarragon—Delicate crunch pairs with subtle sweetness.

Radicchio + Flat-Leaf Parsley or Mint—Bitter edge is tempered by fresh contrast.

Romaine Lettuce + Dill or Basil—Crisp and clean adds bright, sweet notes.

And after a market haul, do this to your herbs and lettuces:

- Store your unwashed leafy greens and herbs in resealable silicone container bags to extend their shelf life and save you money.
- Just before using, thoroughly rinse them under cold water to remove dirt and debris.
- Use a salad spinner to remove as much water as possible. Excess moisture equals soggy greens and hastens decomposition. And dressings won't stick to wet leaves.

RAINBOW VEGGIE PREP

Veggie prep is a great way to build connection in the kitchen. Teach older kids to use a vegetable peeler to make carrot ribbons; a mandoline to thinly slice or julienne (a.k.a. matchsticks) raw dense veggies, such as kohlrabies, beets, and broccoli stems; and a spiralizer for zucchini. Roasted or leftover cooked veggies, such as broccoli, cauliflower, and kohlrabi, add contrast and deep flavor to salads and bowls. Try these salad-ready vegetable cuts:

Beets—Thin slices, cubes, or matchsticks

Bell Peppers—Narrow strips or cubes

Cabbage—Thin shreds

Carrots—Ribbons, matchsticks for crunch, or thin rounds

Celery—Thin diagonal slices

Cherry or Grape Tomatoes—Halved for juicy bursts

Cucumbers—Thin rounds, thicker half-moons, spiralized

Fennel—Shaved thin for a crisp, lightly sweet touch

Green onions—Thin diagonal slices

Radishes—Thin rounds or matchsticks

Snow Peas—Matchsticks for tender snap

Sugar Snap Peas—Halved for crunch

Zucchini—Spiralized

TASTY EXTRAS

Sweet Additions—Fresh and dried fruits, such as blueberries, orange segments, raisins, and cranberries, bring sweet pops that balance earthy veggies. Roasting or grilling fruits, such as peaches, plums, nectarines, pears, and grapes, concentrate their sweetness.

Crunch Craze—Toasted nuts and seeds, such as almonds, pistachios, walnuts, pecans, sunflower, pumpkin, and sesame, are crunchy flavor add-ins and toppers. Keep them fresher longer by storing them in the fridge. If you want to take your salad to the next level, whip up one of these crunchy topping recipes (see pages 77 and 79).

Grain—Grains such as bulgur, quinoa, farro, freekeh, and rice absorb the flavors of dressings, add chewiness and nuttiness, and taste great cold.

Cheese—Add mild, sharp, or tangy cubed, shredded, or grated cheese to salads. For example, use Cheddar, feta, or goat cheese to balance acidity and create an umami depth of flavor and salad harmony. For special touches, try warm seared halloumi (see page 69) or whipped goat cheese (see page 58). Or whip up a batch of easy, make-ahead Black Pepper Parmigiano-Reggiano Crisps (page 79).

Pickle Punch—Fridge pickles—a.k.a. quick pickles—are vinegar-brined make-ahead condiments that don't require canning. Choose hearty vegetables with crunch, such as cucumbers, fennel, red onions, and shallots. Or for a very spicy pickle punch in salads, prep a batch of jalapeño chiles. Store your quick pickles in an airtight container in the refrigerator for up to a week. Their flavor will intensify.

Protein Power—Add protein-packed ingredients, such as roasted or grilled chicken and salmon, cooked shrimp, eggs, cured meats, Crispy Tofu Strips (page 128), chickpeas, and beans to lighter salad creations. You'll boost the flavor and transform your salads into hearty main courses.

Parmigiano-Reggiano Chickpeas

PREP UP TO 1 WEEK AHEAD

MAKES 1½ CUPS

One 15-ounce can chickpeas

2 tablespoons olive oil

½ teaspoon garlic powder

¼ teaspoon kosher salt

¼ cup grated Parmigiano-Reggiano cheese

1. Preheat the oven to 400°F. Line a metal sheet pan with a silicone baking sheet.

2. Drain the chickpeas into a strainer and rinse under cold running water. Spread the chickpeas on a kitchen towel and pat thoroughly dry to ensure they will crisp in the oven.

3. In a small bowl, combine the dried chickpeas, oil, garlic powder, and salt and toss to coat evenly.

4. Spread the chickpeas in a single layer on the prepared sheet pan. Roast the chickpeas, shaking the pan halfway through to ensure even browning, until golden brown and crispy, about 20 minutes.

5. Transfer to a bowl and immediately toss with the cheese. Let cool before adding to salads.

Note: Store the chickpeas in an airtight container at room temperature.

Garlic Croutons

PREP UP TO 1 WEEK AHEAD
MAKES 4 CUPS

4 cups torn bread (any type), in bite-size pieces

3 tablespoons olive oil

2 teaspoons garlic powder

1 teaspoon dried Italian seasoning

1. Preheat the oven to 350°F. Line a metal sheet pan with a silicone baking sheet.

2. Put the bread into a medium bowl. Drizzle with the oil, sprinkle with the garlic powder and Italian seasoning, and toss gently to coat evenly.

3. Spread the bread pieces in a single layer on the prepared sheet pan. Bake, turning the pieces halfway through cooking to ensure even browning, until golden brown, about 10 minutes. Let cool before adding to salads.

Note: Store the croutons in an airtight container at room temperature.

Sweet or Spicy Maple Nut Clusters

PREP UP TO 1 WEEK AHEAD
MAKES 2 CUPS

½ cup pecan halves

½ cup slivered blanched almonds

½ cup cashews

½ cup walnut halves

3 tablespoons maple syrup

¼ teaspoon kosher salt

½ teaspoon ground turmeric (optional)

½ teaspoon smoked paprika (optional)

½ teaspoon curry powder (optional)

1. Line a metal sheet pan with a silicone baking sheet. In a small bowl, mix together the pecan, almonds, cashews, and walnuts.

2. Warm a medium skillet over medium-low heat. Add the nuts and heat gently, stirring constantly, until lightly toasted and fragrant, 1 to 2 minutes. Add the maple syrup and salt. If spicy nut clusters are desired, add the turmeric, paprika, and curry powder along with the salt. Continue stirring until the nuts are well coated with the maple syrup and the pan is dry, about 1 minute more.

3. Remove the skillet from the heat and pour the nuts onto the prepared sheet pan, spreading them in a rough layer. Let cool, then break into small clusters before adding to salads.

Note: Store the clusters in an airtight container at room temperature.

PREP UP TO 1 WEEK AHEAD
MAKES 12 TO 16 CRISPS

1 cup finely grated Parmigiano-Reggiano cheese

½ teaspoon freshly ground black pepper

Black Pepper Parmigiano-Reggiano Crisps

1. Preheat the oven to 400°F. Line a metal sheet pan with a silicone baking sheet.

2. In a small bowl, combine the cheese and pepper and stir to mix well. For each crisp, spoon about 1 tablespoon of the seasoned cheese onto the prepared sheet pan, spacing the mounds about 1 inch apart. You should get 12 to 16 crisps. Slightly flatten each mound into a circle.

3. Bake until golden and bubbly, about 10 minutes. Remove from the oven and let cool before tossing into salads.

Note: Store the crisps in an airtight container at room temperature.

PREP UP TO 1 WEEK AHEAD
MAKES ABOUT 2 CUPS

12 ounces vegetables of choice (such as cucumbers, fennel, red onions, shallots, or jalapeño chiles)

1½ cups apple cider vinegar or distilled white vinegar

1½ cups hot water

3 tablespoons kosher salt

2 tablespoons pickling spice

Any Quick Pickle

1. Trim your choice of vegetables as needed, then, using a chef's knife or mandoline, cut into slices. Cut vegetables such as cucumbers and fennel into uniform slices about ¼ inch thick. If using chiles, shallots, or red onions, slice into thin rings.

2. In a medium bowl, whisk together the vinegar, hot water, salt, and pickling spice until the salt dissolves.

3. Add the vegetables and toss gently to coat evenly. Set aside for 15 minutes, stirring occasionally, then serve.

Note: Store the quick pickle in an airtight container in the fridge.

PREP-AHEAD ELEMENT(S)

SERVES 4 TO 6

Smoked Salmon Cobb with Jammy Eggs and Garlic Herb Dressing

4 eggs

8 ounces (6 slices) thick-cut bacon

GARLIC HERB DRESSING

1 cup plain full-fat Greek yogurt

2 tablespoons Dijon mustard

¼ cup extra-virgin olive oil

1 garlic clove, minced

½ teaspoon garlic powder

Juice of 1 lime

¼ teaspoon kosher salt

Pinch of freshly ground black pepper

¼ cup packed finely chopped mixed fresh herbs (such as dill, flat-leaf parsley, cilantro, chives, and tarragon, in any combination)

This glorious Cobb salad leans into spring with sunny, jammy eggs, hot smoked salmon, and crunchy raw asparagus and radishes, along with crisp bacon and creamy avocado. The yogurt-based herb dressing is garlicky and flush with herbs. Use leftover dressing as a dip for raw or roasted veggies. For such a seemingly indulgent salad, you can prep the components in advance, making it fast to assemble for a special brunch get-together.

1. *Prep the eggs:* Fill a large saucepan three-fourths full with water and bring to a boil over high heat. Using a slotted spoon and working quickly, gently lower the eggs, one at a time, into the boiling water. Set a timer for 8 minutes to cook the eggs. While the eggs are cooking, fill a medium bowl with ice water.

2. Ding—the timer went off! Use the slotted spoon to transfer the eggs to the ice bath. Let the eggs sit until totally cool, about 15 minutes. Stopping the cooking process is a must to get the jammy center. Drain the eggs, then carefully crack and peel them. Cut them in half and set aside cut-side up—wow, so golden!

3. *Prep the bacon:* Preheat the oven to 400°F. Line a metal sheet pan with a silicone baking sheet. Arrange the bacon slices in a single layer on the prepared sheet pan, transfer to the oven, and cook until crispy, 10 to 12 minutes. Remove from the oven. Once the bacon is cool enough to handle, finely chop it and set aside.

4. *Make the dressing:* In a medium bowl, whisk together the yogurt, mustard, oil, minced garlic, garlic powder, lime juice, salt, and pepper until creamy. Stir in the herbs.

5. *Assemble the salad:* Pour about ¼ cup of the dressing into a medium bowl. Add the lettuce and toss gently to coat

Continued

Smoked Salmon Cobb with Jammy Eggs and Garlic Herb Dressing, continued

SALAD

1 head Bibb lettuce, cored and leaves separated and torn into bite-size pieces

4 ounces hot-smoked salmon, flaked into large chunks

½ English cucumber, halved lengthwise, seeded, and diced

10 asparagus spears, woody ends trimmed and thinly sliced on the diagonal, or 4 hearts of palm (from one 14-ounce can), drained and sliced lengthwise

4 green onions, light green and white parts only, finely chopped

6 radishes, thinly sliced

1 avocado, halved, pitted, peeled, and cubed

Freshly cracked black pepper for finishing

Leaves picked from fresh soft herbs (such as flat-leaf parsley, cilantro, dill, and/or tarragon) for garnish

evenly. The water-rich lettuce will dilute the thick dressing. Arrange the dressed lettuce in a bed on a large serving platter. Nestle the salmon, egg halves, chopped bacon, cucumber, asparagus, green onions, radishes, and avocado in the crevices and folds of the lettuce. Top the salad with a few grinds of the pepper mill and then with the herbs. Serve the remaining dressing in a bowl on the side for drizzling over the top at the table. Dig in!

Notes: Make the eggs up to 1 day ahead. Store in an airtight container in the fridge, but don't peel them until ready to use.

Cook the bacon up to 2 days ahead. Store in an airtight container in the fridge. Warm chopped bacon in a skillet over medium-low heat, stirring often, for 1 minute.

Make the dressing up to 1 day ahead, omitting the herbs. Store in an airtight container in the fridge. Stir in the herbs just before serving.

Weeknight Winners

"Buy cheese when it is on sale, grate it, and freeze. Add a little cornstarch to it and it won't clump together. This works great when you need it for a casserole; just open your container, and take out what you need."

—JOAN N.,
33 YEARS SELLING TUPPERWARE PRODUCTS

Let's conquer the week with inspired, flavor-packed dinners that come together fast. We know everyone's meal prep style is different, so we've packed this chapter with flexible make-ahead tips to fit your busy schedule, from making a batch of pork meatballs for zesty Pork Meatball Rolls with Pickled Veg and Cilantro Mayo (page 99) to prepping and storing shredded chicken, refried beans, and brisket to have on hand for Crunchy Tostada Night (page 105) or for spinning into melts, burritos, kids' meals, and more. You've got to love meal prep that does double or triple duty! And no worries if you have only a few minutes. Prepare delicious sauces like pistachio pesto (see page 95) and lemon caper tartar sauce (see page 115) or a delectable side of kale au gratin (see page 89) ahead of time to help you tackle busy nights.

- Use the **SUPERSONIC CHOPPER EXTRA** to make the pesto for Pistachio Pesto Pasta with Tinned Fish (page 95). Add the ingredients as directed and pull the cord until a loose sauce forms.
- Leftovers? Freeze them for later! **VENT 'N SERVE** containers can go from the freezer to the microwave, saving time and energy and reducing plastic wrap and paper waste.
- Use the **MICROWAVE PRESSURE COOKER** to cook Vegetarian Refried Beans (page 108) in a fraction of the stovetop time.

PREP-AHEAD ELEMENT(S)

FREEZER-FRIENDLY
UP TO 3 MONTHS

SERVES 4

Fish and "Chips" with Kale au Gratin

No batter, no frying—this fish and "chips" goes light and easy! Firm white fish fillets are coated in dill mayo to lock in moisture and then topped with crushed salt-and-vinegar potato chips for a crunchy, yummy crust. Pair it with a side of creamy kale that feels luxurious but can be prepped ahead and baked later. It's an easy weeknight meal that feels like a special occasion.

KALE AU GRATIN

- 4 tablespoons unsalted butter
- ¼ cup all-purpose flour
- 3 cups whole or 1-percent milk
- 1 cup heavy cream
- 4 ounces cream cheese, at room temperature
- 1 teaspoon smoked paprika
- 1 teaspoon kosher salt
- ½ teaspoon freshly ground black pepper
- ½ cup grated Parmigiano-Reggiano cheese
- 2 pounds Lacinato kale, stems and ribs removed and leaves torn or chopped into bite-size pieces

FISH

- ½ cup mayonnaise
- 1 teaspoon Dijon mustard
- 2 tablespoons finely chopped fresh dill
- Four 6-ounce skinless firm white fish fillets (such as cod, haddock, bass, or snapper), each about 1 inch thick
- Kosher salt and freshly ground black or ground white pepper
- ¾ cup finely crushed salt-and-vinegar potato chips (from about 2½ cups chips)

1. Position one rack in the upper third of the oven and one rack in the lower third of the oven, then preheat the oven to 375°F. Line a metal sheet pan with a silicone baking sheet.

2. *Make the sauce for the gratin:* In a medium saucepan, melt the butter over medium heat. Slowly add the flour while whisking constantly, then continue whisking until a smooth, golden paste forms, about 1 minute. Slowly whisk the milk, cream, cream cheese, paprika, salt, pepper, and ¼ cup of the Parmigiano-Reggiano into the flour-butter paste, making sure you reach the bottom and sides of the pan and the mixture is lump-free. Bring the sauce to a low simmer and cook, whisking continuously, until smooth and thickened, about 5 minutes. Remove from the heat.

3. Put the kale into a large mixing bowl. Slowly pour the sauce over the kale and toss until the kale wilts. Transfer the kale to a 9 by 13-inch baking dish. Scatter the remaining ¼ cup Parmigiano-Reggiano evenly over the top. Place on the lower rack of the oven and bake uncovered until bubbly and the top is browned, about 30 minutes.

4. *Meanwhile, prep the fish:* In a small bowl, stir together the mayonnaise, mustard, and dill, mixing well. Arrange the fish fillets in a single layer on the prepared sheet pan and season on both sides with salt and pepper. Using a silicone spatula, spread about 2 tablespoons of the mayonnaise mixture on top of each fillet, covering it evenly. Top each fillet with 3 tablespoons of the crushed potato chips, spreading them evenly.

Continued

Fish and "Chips" with Kale au Gratin, continued

5. When the gratin has baked for about 20 minutes, place the sheet pan with the fish on the upper rack of the oven and bake until the fish is opaque and flakes when tested with a fork and the potato chips are toasted, about 10 minutes.

6. Transfer the fish to a serving platter and serve with the kale alongside.

Note: To freeze the kale au gratin, prep ahead through step 3, omitting the final ¼ cup grated Parmigiano-Reggiano cheese. Transfer the kale mixture to an airtight container and freeze. Thaw in the fridge before transferring to a baking dish. Garnish with the remaining ¼ cup Parmigiano-Reggiano cheese and bake.

PREP-AHEAD ELEMENT(S)

SERVES 4 TO 6

Spicy Drumsticks with Potatoes and Mint Yogurt Dressing

DRUMSTICKS

2 pounds skin-on chicken drumsticks, scored (see headnote)

2 teaspoons kosher salt

SPICY MARINADE

⅓ cup olive oil

1 tablespoon red wine vinegar

1-inch piece fresh ginger, peeled and minced, or 1 teaspoon ginger paste

1½ teaspoons Calabrian chili paste or harissa paste

10 garlic cloves, roughly chopped

1 small red onion, roughly chopped

2 or 3 flat-leaf parsley sprigs

1 red bell pepper, seeded and roughly chopped

2 tablespoons tomato paste

2 tablespoons dried Italian seasoning

2 teaspoons smoked paprika

1 teaspoon kosher salt

Pinch of freshly ground black pepper

Infuse hearty chicken drumsticks with a heady marinade inspired by garlicky, vinegary Portuguese peri-peri sauce that melts into a mouthwatering sauce for serving. Pair them with potatoes that cook simultaneously on the top oven rack and use dollops of cooling mint-flecked yogurt to balance the heat for a feast with mostly hands-off cooking time. To help the chicken more fully absorb the marinade, score the meatiest part of each drumstick with two or three slashes.

1. *Salt the drumsticks:* Put the drumsticks into a large bowl. Season all over with the salt and set aside.

2. *Make the marinade:* In a blender, combine the oil, vinegar, ginger, chili paste, garlic, onion, parsley, bell pepper, tomato paste, Italian seasoning, paprika, salt, and black pepper and blend until smooth.

3. Pour the marinade over the drumsticks, then spoon the marinade over the drumsticks to smother them well. Cover and refrigerate for at least 6 hours or up to overnight.

4. *When ready to cook:* Position one rack in the upper third of the oven and one rack in the lower third of the oven, then preheat the oven to 400°F. Line a metal sheet pan with a silicone baking sheet.

5. *Prep the potatoes:* Put the potatoes into a large bowl. Add the oil, garlic powder, salt, and pepper and toss to coat evenly. Squeeze the juice from the lemon half over the top and toss again. Arrange the potatoes cut-side down on the prepared sheet pan.

6. *Cook the drumsticks and potatoes:* Arrange the drumsticks in a single layer in a large roasting pan and pour in the marinade. Place the sheet pan with the potatoes on the top rack and the roasting pan with the drumsticks on the lower rack in the oven. Roast the potatoes until tender and browned on the bottom and the chicken until the juices run clear and the marinade transforms into a bubbling sauce, about 1 hour.

Continued

Spicy Drumsticks with Potatoes and Mint Yogurt Dressing, continued

POTATOES

2 pounds red potatoes, scrubbed and quartered if large, halved if small

2 tablespoons olive oil

1 teaspoon garlic powder

½ teaspoon kosher salt

Pinch of freshly ground black pepper

½ medium lemon

MINT YOGURT DRESSING

½ cup plain full-fat Greek yogurt

1 teaspoon garlic powder

½ teaspoon fresh lime juice

¼ cup finely chopped fresh mint

7. *Meanwhile, make the mint yogurt dressing:* In a small bowl, stir together the yogurt, garlic powder, lime juice, and mint. Cover and refrigerate until ready to use.

8. Transfer the chicken and potatoes to a large platter. Serve family-style, covered with spoonfuls of the pan sauce and with the mint yogurt alongside.

Notes: Make the spicy marinade up to 2 days ahead. Store in an airtight container in the fridge.

Make the mint yogurt dressing up to 1 day ahead. Store in an airtight container in the fridge.

Pistachio Pesto Pasta with Tinned Fish

8 ounces fusilli or other short pasta

¾ cup Pesto (recipe follows), plus more if needed

Two 5-ounce cans tuna or sardines packed in olive oil, drained

2 tablespoons medium capers packed in salt, well rinsed, or in brine, drained

½ medium lemon

In this twist on pasta with pesto, savory tinned tuna and salty capers—a traditional pairing—are added along with the pistachio pesto, which brings natural sweetness and creaminess while being more budget friendly than traditional pine nuts. Short pastas such as fusilli or cavatappi have grooves or ridges that the clingy pesto can hug.

1. *Cook the pasta:* Bring a large pot of generously salted water to boil over high heat. Add the pasta and cook according to the directions on the package for al dente pasta. Before draining, use a measuring cup to scoop out about ½ cup of the pasta water and set aside. Drain the pasta and return it to the now-empty pot.

2. *Bring the flavors together:* Add the pesto to the pasta and return the pan to medium heat. Use tongs to gently coat the pasta, adding splashes of the reserved pasta water to loosen the pesto as needed, about 30 seconds. If the pesto looks too sparse, add a little more and toss to mix. Add the tuna and capers and continue to toss until the tuna is warmed through, about 2 minutes more. Squeeze the juice from the lemon half over the top and toss once more. Serve now!

Continued

Pistachio Pesto Pasta with Tinned Fish, continued

Pesto

PREP UP TO 1-WEEK AHEAD

FREEZER-FRIENDLY UP TO 3 MONTHS

MAKES ABOUT 1¼ CUPS

¼ cup salted roasted pistachios

1 garlic clove

3 cups packed fresh basil leaves (from 2 large bunches)

¼ cup grated Parmigiano-Reggiano cheese

¼ teaspoon kosher salt

¾ cup extra-virgin olive oil, plus more as needed

Besides pasta, pesto is wonderful on sandwiches or toast or added to an omelet—yum! Note: Transfer the pesto to an airtight container, smooth over the top, and drizzle with a thin layer of extra-virgin olive oil before sealing and storing in the fridge. This helps preserve its color and flavor. Store the pesto in an airtight container in the fridge. For longer storage, freeze the pesto in smaller portions for up to 3 months.

In a food processor, combine the pistachios and garlic and pulse until the pistachios are finely ground and the garlic is finely minced. Add the basil, cheese, salt, and oil and blend until smooth. If the pesto seems too thick, drizzle in a little more oil and blend until smooth. Use right away or store as directed in the headnote.

PREP-AHEAD ELEMENT(S)

FREEZER-FRIENDLY
UP TO 3 MONTHS

MAKES 4 6-INCH SANDWICHES & EXTRA MEATBALLS

Pork Meatball Rolls with Pickled Veg and Cilantro Mayo

PORK MEATBALLS

2 pounds ground pork

2 teaspoons kosher salt

½ teaspoon freshly ground black pepper

1 tablespoon soy sauce

2 teaspoons ginger paste

1 bunch green onions, white parts only, finely chopped

2 teaspoons toasted sesame oil, plus more for cooking

TERIYAKI SAUCE

½ cup packed light brown sugar

¾ cup soy sauce

⅓ cup water

¼ cup rice vinegar

½ teaspoon garlic powder

CILANTRO MAYO

½ cup mayonnaise

½ small shallot, finely chopped

¼ cup finely chopped fresh cilantro

½ teaspoon kosher salt

SANDWICHES

One 24-inch-long baguette

¾ cup quick pickled vegetables (see page 79) of choice (such as red onion, cucumber, carrot, bell pepper, or jalapeño chile, or a colorful mix)

½ cup shredded green cabbage or romaine or other crisp lettuce

Inspired by the beloved Vietnamese bánh mì sandwich, these rolls combine savory pork meatballs with pickled vegetables all layered on a toasted baguette for a zesty, crunchy bite. Meatballs are a terrific make-ahead protein and seasoning them with green onions and ginger brings fresh flavor to a comforting standby. For another meal, serve the extra meatballs over rice, over a veggie stir-fry, or in a lettuce wrap with pickled veggies and sesame seeds.

1. *Make the meatballs:* In a large bowl, combine the pork, salt, pepper, soy sauce, ginger, green onions, and the 2 teaspoons oil, mixing well. Cover and refrigerate for 20 minutes.

2. *Meanwhile, make the teriyaki sauce:* In a medium bowl, whisk together the brown sugar, soy sauce, water, vinegar, and garlic powder until the sugar dissolves.

3. When ready to roll the meatballs, have ready a large plate. Stir to make sure the mixture is well mixed, then with lightly wet hands, form golf-ball-size meatballs (about 2 tablespoons each) and place on the plate. You should have twenty-four to twenty-seven meatballs.

4. *Cook the meatballs:* Have a large plate ready. In a large skillet, heat 1 tablespoon sesame oil over high heat until shimmering. Add as many meatballs to the pan in a single layer as will fit without crowding and cook until browned on the bottom, about 3 minutes. Flip and cook until browned on the second side, about 3 minutes more. Transfer to the plate. Repeat with the remaining meatballs in one or two batches as needed, wiping out the pan and heating 1 tablespoon sesame oil before adding a new batch. Once all the meatballs are browned, return them to the skillet, add the teriyaki sauce, and bring to a boil. Turn down the heat to a simmer and cook undisturbed until the sauce thickens slightly and the meatballs are cooked through, 5 to 7 minutes.

Continued

Pork Meatball Rolls with Pickled Veg and Cilantro Mayo, continued

5. *Meanwhile, make the mayonnaise:* In a medium bowl, stir together the mayonnaise, shallot, cilantro, and salt, mixing well.

6. Preheat the oven to 325°F.

7. *To assemble the sandwiches:* Using a serrated knife, split the baguette in half horizontally, stopping just short of cutting all the way through. Using your fingers or a small knife, scoop out some of the crumb from both halves to make a trough for the meatballs. (Save the bread crumb for making the Garlic Croutons on page 78.) Place the baguette directly on the oven rack and bake until lightly toasted, about 10 minutes. Remove from the oven, let cool slightly, and spread both cut sides of the bread with the cilantro mayo. Place a thin layer of cabbage on the bottom half, followed by a layer of pickled veggies. Line up twelve meatballs along the length of the baguette. Close the baguette and squish down on the top half. Using the serrated knife, cut the baguette into four 6-inch-long sandwiches, using every third meatball as a guide. Eat now!

Notes: Roll the meatballs up to 3 months ahead. Uncooked meatballs freeze beautifully! Arrange them in a single layer on a metal sheet pan lined with a silicone baking sheet and freeze for 2 hours, then transfer to a freezer-safe container and return to the freezer. Thaw the meatballs overnight in the fridge before cooking.

Cook the meatballs up to 3 days ahead. Store in an airtight container in the fridge. To reheat, arrange them on a silicone baking sheet and drizzle the tops with olive oil. Reheat in the oven at 350°F for 15 minutes.

PREP UP TO
2 DAYS AHEAD

FREEZER-FRIENDLY
UP TO 3 MONTHS

SERVES 4 TO 6

Moussaka-Style Eggplant Stacks

EGGPLANT

2 pounds eggplant, peeled and sliced crosswise into ½-inch-thick rounds (18 to 24 rounds)

Kosher salt

Olive oil for brushing

BEEF SAUCE

2 teaspoons kosher salt

1 teaspoon ground cinnamon

1 teaspoon ground cardamom

½ teaspoon garlic powder

¼ teaspoon ground coriander

1 teaspoon olive oil

1 small onion, finely diced

1 pound lean ground beef

1 cup crushed canned tomatoes

YOGURT SAUCE

2 cups plain full-fat Greek yogurt

½ cup heavy cream

2 egg yolks, lightly beaten (see Notes, page 105)

½ teaspoon ground nutmeg

¼ cup grated Parmigiano-Reggiano cheese

Torn fresh mint leaves for garnish

These individually portioned moussaka-inspired eggplant stacks make prepping, storing, and serving far simpler than for the traditional casserole. And a no-cook yogurt sauce cuts the work of the classic béchamel sauce—a hack that yields luscious results! The beef sauce has the warm spice flavors of cinnamon and cardamom that everyone will love. And if the kids aren't into eggplant (yet!), we got you: make a double batch of the beef sauce and serve it with some pasta shells or elbows for a sure-to-be-a-hit kids' dinner.

1. *Prep the eggplant:* Position one rack in the upper third of the oven and one rack in the lower third of oven, then preheat the oven to 450°F. Line two metal sheet pans with clean kitchen towels. Arrange the eggplant rounds in a single layer, not overlapping, on the prepared sheet pans. Generously sprinkle with salt and let sit for 20 minutes.

2. *Meanwhile, make the beef sauce:* In a small bowl, stir together the salt, cinnamon, cardamom, garlic powder, and coriander and set aside. In a medium skillet, heat the oil over medium-high heat until shimmering. Add the onion and cook, stirring often, until lightly golden, about 3 minutes. Add the beef and season with the reserved spice mixture. Cook, stirring and breaking up the beef with the back of a wooden spoon, until browned, about 4 minutes. Stir in the tomatoes and continue cooking until the liquid in the pan reduces slightly, about 3 minutes more. Remove from the heat and set aside.

3. *Precook the eggplant rounds:* Pat the eggplant rounds and sheet pans dry of any water the eggplant released. Line each sheet pan with a silicone baking sheet. Arrange the eggplant rounds in a single layer on the prepared sheet pans and brush on both sides with oil. Place one pan on the upper rack and the second pan on the lower rack and roast the eggplant rounds, flipping them halfway through the cooking time, until lightly golden and fork-tender, 16 to 20 minutes. Remove from the oven and set aside. Lower the oven temperature to 350°F.

Continued

Moussaka-Style Eggplant Stacks, continued

4. *Make the yogurt sauce:* In a medium bowl, stir together the yogurt, cream, eggs, nutmeg, and cheese, mixing well.

5. *Assemble and bake the stacks:* Spread a thin layer of beef sauce on the bottom of a 9 by 13-inch lasagna or baking dish. Arrange the six largest eggplant rounds in a single layer in the bottom of the dish. Top each round with about 1½ tablespoons of the beef sauce, followed by about 2 tablespoons of the yogurt sauce. Stack another, smaller eggplant round on top of each yogurt layer, then top with beef sauce and yogurt sauce. Repeat the layers of eggplant, beef sauce, and yogurt sauce until each stack has three or four eggplant rounds and finishes with a layer of yogurt sauce.

6. Bake the stacks until the tops are golden brown and bubbly, about 30 minutes. Allow to rest for 10 minutes, then garnish with mint and serve.

Notes: Save the egg whites for making Chocolate-Dipped Coconut Macaroons (page 194).

Store the stacks covered in the fridge. Reheat uncovered in the oven at 350°F for 25 to 30 minutes. To freeze for later, assemble the stacks but do not bake. Thaw in the fridge overnight, then bake as directed.

Crunchy Tostada Night

SERVES 6 TO 8

Tostadas—crisp Mexican corn tortillas—are ideal for piling with refried beans, shredded brisket or chicken, cheese, fresh and pickled veggies, vibrant salsa, and silky lime-infused crema. But don't stop at tostadas. The same bases can be built into other dishes, turning tostada prep into meals for the entire week. Hooray!

BASE

18 to 24 store-bought tostada shells (plan on 3 shells per person)

3 to 5 cups your choice of shredded adobo chicken (page 112), Buffalo chicken (page 112), brisket (page 109), or refried beans (108)

TOPPING SUGGESTIONS

Assorted fresh or quick pickled vegetables (page 79) of choice (such as red onions and radishes)

Thin avocado slices

Thinly sliced celery stalks

Halved cherry tomatoes

Store-bought salsa or Pico de Gallo (recipe follows)

Chopped fresh cilantro

Crumbled Cotija and/or blue cheese

Thinly sliced jalapeño chiles

Shredded Cheddar cheese

Shredded lettuce or green cabbage

Sliced bell peppers (any color) or Stuffed Mini Peppers (recipe follows)

Sour cream or Lime Crema (recipe follows)

HOW TO SET UP

- Get ahead by prepping your preferred toppings in advance. Label each container and store the containers in your fridge or freezer, following the get-ahead notes for each recipe.
- When ready to serve, set out the proteins and toppings in colorful serving bowls and pile the tostadas onto a serving platter.

Lime Crema

PREP UP TO 2 DAYS AHEAD

MAKES 1 CUP

1 cup full-fat sour cream

1 teaspoon garlic powder

¼ teaspoon kosher salt

Grated zest and juice of 2 small limes

Traditional Mexican crema has a thinner consistency than sour cream, but adding fresh lime juice to full-fat sour cream thins the sour cream and brings tangy, bright flavor.

In a medium bowl, stir together the sour cream, garlic powder, salt, and lime zest and juice. Enjoy now drizzled over tostadas.

Note: Store the crema in an airtight container in the fridge.

Pico de Gallo

MAKES ABOUT 2 CUPS

1 pint cherry tomatoes (10 to 12 ounces), quartered

¼ cup finely chopped red onion (from ¼ medium onion)

2 tablespoons finely chopped fresh cilantro

2 tablespoons finely chopped fresh flat-leaf parsley

1 jalapeño chile, seeded and finely chopped

½ teaspoon kosher salt

Juice of ¼ lime

When freshly made, this salsa bursts with zippy flavor and gorgeous color. It's especially delicious over brisket tostadas to balance the rich meat.

In a medium bowl, stir together the tomatoes, onion, cilantro, parsley, jalapeño, salt, and lime juice. Cover and refrigerate for 1 hour before serving as a topping for tostadas or a dip for tortilla chips.

Note: Make the salsa up to 4 hours before serving. Store covered in the fridge.

Stuffed Mini Peppers

PREP UP TO 1 DAY AHEAD

MAKES ABOUT 24 PEPPERS

4 ounces cream cheese, at room temperature

½ cup plain or marinated feta cheese, at room temperature

12 to 14 mini peppers, cut in half, stems left intact and membranes and seeds discarded

The roasted sweetness and creamy cheese filling of these stuffed peppers pair with every base and contrast perfectly with the crunch of the tostada. Plus, they look so cute!

1. Preheat the oven to 400°F. Line a metal sheet pan with a silicone baking sheet.

2. In a small bowl, use a fork to mash together the cream cheese and feta cheese until well mixed and smooth.

3. Using a small spoon, stuff each pepper half with the cheese mixture, using the back of the spoon to smooth the top so the filling is level with the sides of the pepper. Arrange the peppers, filled-side up and close together, on the prepared sheet pan.

4. Roast until the cheese is melty and the edges of the peppers are blistered, 15 to 20 minutes. Enjoy warm or at room temperature.

Note: Prep the peppers up to 1 day ahead without roasting. Store in an airtight container in the fridge until ready to roast.

PREP UP TO
3 DAYS AHEAD

FREEZER-FRIENDLY
UP TO 3 MONTHS

MAKES ABOUT 6 CUPS

Vegetarian Refried Beans

1 tablespoon plus 1 teaspoon olive oil

1 medium yellow onion, diced

2 medium red or green bell peppers, seeded and diced

3 garlic cloves, minced

1 tablespoon ground cumin

1 teaspoon chili powder

3 cups dried pinto beans or black beans, soaked overnight in water to cover, rinsed, and drained

1 cup crushed tomatoes

4 cups low-sodium vegetable broth, plus more if needed

Kosher salt

These from-scratch vegetarian (and vegan!) refried beans are packed with deep, bold flavor that canned beans can't match. Plus, you can control the texture—from chunky to silky smooth. Make a big batch for tostadas, breakfast quesadillas, or Fiesta Dip (page 213). Be sure to soak the beans overnight. It softens them for even cooking and results in creamier beans.

1. *Build flavor:* In a medium skillet, heat 1 tablespoon of the oil over medium heat until shimmering. Add the onion and cook, stirring often, until lightly golden, about 5 minutes. Add the bell peppers and continue cooking, stirring often, until softened, about 3 minutes. Add the remaining 1 teaspoon oil, the garlic, cumin, and chili powder. Continue cooking, stirring often, until the garlic is soft and the spices are fragrant, about 30 seconds more. Remove from the heat.

2. *Cook the beans:* In a large pot with a lid, combine the onion-pepper mixture, beans, tomatoes, broth, and 1 tablespoon salt and bring to a boil over high heat. Turn down the heat to a low simmer, cover with the lid ajar, and cook until the beans are tender, about 2 hours. The beans will absorb most of the liquid. Remove from the heat.

3. Working in batches, transfer the beans and ¼ cup of their cooking liquid to a food processor and process to your desired consistency, adding more cooking liquid or broth if needed for blending. Season to taste with salt.

Note: Let the beans cool completely then store in an airtight container in the fridge. To freeze the beans, divide into smaller portions, if desired, and cover with some of the cooking liquid or with additional broth if needed. Thaw overnight in the fridge before reheating on the stovetop over low heat.

PREP UP TO
3 DAYS AHEAD

FREEZER-FRIENDLY
UP TO 3 MONTHS

SERVES 8

Slow-Cooked Brisket and Onions

Here's a low-key prep plan: Quickly season the brisket on Friday and let it rest in the fridge overnight. On Saturday morning, sear it, then pop it into the oven for low-and-slow hands-off cooking in a roasting pan. Shred and use for meals such as Crunchy Tostadas (page 105) or Brisket Stroganoff (page 169).

SWEET SPICE MIX

3 tablespoons brown sugar

1½ tablespoons smoked paprika

1½ tablespoons garlic powder

1½ tablespoons onion powder

1½ teaspoons mustard powder

BRISKET AND ONIONS

4 tablespoons vegetable oil

3 medium yellow onions, thinly sliced

3 garlic cloves, thinly sliced

One 3- to 4-pound flat-cut brisket (¼- to ½-inch fat cap)

4 teaspoons kosher salt

2 teaspoons freshly ground black pepper

4 cups low-sodium beef broth, plus more if needed

¼ cup Worcestershire sauce or soy sauce

¼ cup apple cider vinegar

1. *Make the spice mix:* In a small bowl, combine the sugar, paprika, garlic powder, onion powder, and mustard powder.

2. *Prep the brisket and onions:* In a large skillet, heat 2 tablespoons of the oil over medium heat until shimmering. Add the onions and cook, stirring often, until softened, 5 to 7 minutes. Add the garlic and cook, stirring, until fragrant, about 30 seconds more. Transfer the garlic and onions to a 6-quart roasting pan with an oven-safe lid. Preheat the oven to 325°F.

3. Place the brisket on a cutting board. Generously season on all sides with the salt and pepper, followed by the reserved sweet spice mix.

4. Heat the remaining 2 tablespoons oil in the now-empty skillet over medium heat until shimmering. Transfer the seasoned brisket, fat-side down, to the skillet and sear until the fat renders and a crust forms, 8 to 10 minutes. Using tongs and a spatula, carefully flip the brisket and sear on the other side until deeply browned, about 8 minutes more.

5. Transfer the brisket, fat-side up, to the pan with the onions. Pour the broth into the pan until it comes up the sides of the brisket, then add the Worcestershire sauce and vinegar. Cover the pan, transfer to the oven, and braise until an instant-read thermometer inserted into the thickest part registers 195°F or until it's tender enough to shred easily with a fork, 5½ to 6 hours.

6. Transfer the brisket to a cutting board to rest for 30 minutes before serving.

Note: Store the brisket in an airtight container in the fridge or freeze in smaller portions. Thaw overnight in the fridge, then cover with some of the onions and broth and reheat in the oven at 325°F until warmed through, about 20 minutes.

PREP UP TO
3 DAYS AHEAD

FREEZER-FRIENDLY
UP TO 3 MONTHS

MAKES ABOUT 6 CUPS

Shredded Buffalo or Adobo Chicken

- 4 cups water
- ¼ cup kosher salt
- 2 bay leaves
- Grated zest of 1 lemon
- 2 pounds boneless, skinless chicken breasts
- 4 cups low-sodium chicken broth, plus more if needed
- Buffalo Sauce or Adobo Sauce for serving (recipes follow), optional

Soaking chicken breasts in seasoned salt water (brining) before cooking boosts flavor and texture, making the chicken tender and easy to shred. Enjoy this chicken plain in a kale Caesar salad (page 61) or toss it in Buffalo or adobo sauce (recipes follow) for tostadas (page 105), quesadillas, or sliders.

1. *Brine the chicken:* In a large, nonmetal bowl, combine the water and salt and stir until the salt dissolves. Add the bay leaves, lemon zest, and chicken. Cover and refrigerate for 1½ to 2 hours.

2. *Cook the chicken:* Remove the chicken from the brine—discard the brine—and transfer the chicken to a medium saucepan with a lid. Pour in the broth. It should cover the chicken by 1 inch. Bring to a boil over a medium-high heat, then turn down the heat to a low simmer. Cover with the lid ajar, and simmer gently until cooked through and tender, 20 to 22 minutes.

3. *Shred the chicken:* Remove the chicken from the broth, transfer to a large bowl, and let rest for 10 minutes. Reserve the broth for soup. Using two forks, shred the chicken. Eat it plain or dress it with the Buffalo or adobo sauce. If using a sauce, toss together with tongs over low heat until the chicken is thoroughly coated in the sauce and warmed through, 3 to 5 minutes.

Note: Store the chicken, dressed in the sauce, in an airtight container in the fridge. To freeze the shredded chicken, divide it into smaller portions, if desired. Thaw overnight in the fridge before reheating in the microwave at 50 percent power for 2 minutes or more. Or warm on the stovetop with Buffalo or adobo sauce.

Buffalo Sauce

PREP UP TO 1 WEEK AHEAD

MAKES ABOUT 1¼ CUPS

- 1 cup unsalted butter
- 1 cup hot sauce, any type
- 2 teaspoons honey
- 2 tablespoons distilled white vinegar
- 1 teaspoon garlic powder
- ¼ teaspoon kosher salt

The punch of heat in this sauce is balanced with a touch of honey. If you make the sauce in advance, reheat over low heat, gently whisking until smooth and warmed through.

In a large skillet, melt the butter over medium-low heat. Gently whisk in the hot sauce, honey, vinegar, garlic powder, and salt. Turn down the heat to low and cook, whisking continuously, until the flavors are melded, about 5 minutes.

Note: Store the Buffalo sauce in an airtight container in the fridge.

Adobo Sauce

PREP UP TO 1 WEEK AHEAD

MAKES ABOUT 1¼ CUPS

- 1 cup tomato puree or tomato passata
- ½ cup low-sodium chicken broth
- 1 to 2 chipotle chiles in adobo sauce, or more if you like it hot!
- 2 teaspoons smoked paprika
- 1 teaspoon ground cumin
- 2 teaspoons unsweetened cocoa powder
- 1 teaspoon kosher salt

Customize this rich, tangy sauce with as much smoky heat as you can handle by adding more chipotle chiles. If you make the sauce in advance, reheat over low heat, gently whisking until smooth and warmed through.

In a blender, combine the tomato puree, broth, chiles, paprika, cumin, cocoa powder, and salt and blend until smooth. Transfer the sauce to a large skillet and place over medium-high heat. Bring the sauce to a boil, then turn down the heat to low and simmer until the flavors are melded, about 8 minutes.

Note: Store the adobo sauce in an airtight container in the fridge.

PREP UP TO
1 DAY AHEAD

FREEZER-FRIENDLY
UP TO 3 MONTHS

MAKES 8 4-OUNCE CAKES

Herb and Potato Fish Cakes with Lemon Caper Tartar Sauce

LEMON CAPER TARTAR SAUCE

1 cup mayonnaise

¼ cup capers packed in salt, well rinsed, or in brine, drained, and finely chopped

Juice of ½ lemon

¼ teaspoon freshly ground black pepper

2 tablespoons finely chopped fresh flat-leaf parsley

FISH CAKES

1½ pounds skinless firm white fish fillets (such as cod, haddock, or grouper)

Kosher salt and freshly ground black or ground white pepper

1 pound russet potatoes, unpeeled, cut into 2-inch pieces

1 egg, beaten

2 tablespoons mayonnaise

1 bunch green onions, light green and white parts, finely chopped

1 cup finely chopped mixed fresh soft herbs (such as dill, flat-leaf parsley, and tarragon)

Olive oil for cooking

Flaky white fish, mashed potatoes, green onions, and an abundance of fragrant herbs are combined to create these comforting, crispy panfried fish cakes. We serve them with a caper-studded lemony tartar sauce for dipping. The mild flavor is perfect for kids too!

1. *Make the tartar sauce:* In a small bowl, stir together the mayonnaise, capers, lemon juice, pepper, and parsley. Cover and refrigerate until ready to use.

2. *Prep the fish:* Preheat the oven to 375°F. Line a metal sheet pan with a silicone baking sheet. Arrange the fish fillets on the prepared sheet pan and season on both sides with salt and pepper. Bake until the fish is opaque and flakes easily when tested with a fork, about 10 minutes. Remove from the oven and gently flake the fish into large pieces. Set aside.

3. *Meanwhile, cook the potatoes:* In a medium saucepan, combine the potatoes with water to cover by 2 inches and 1 tablespoon salt. Bring to a boil over high heat and cook until fork-tender, about 20 minutes. Drain the potatoes into a colander and leave in the colander for 5 minutes to drain excess water. Transfer the potatoes to the now-empty pot and, using a masher, mash the potatoes until smooth.

4. Add the egg, mayonnaise, green onions, herbs, and 1 teaspoon salt to the mashed potatoes and stir to combine. Gently fold the reserved flaked fish into the potatoes, distributing it evenly. Transfer the mixture of a large bowl, cover, and refrigerate for at least 1 hour or up to overnight.

5. *Form the fish cakes:* Have ready a large plate. To form each cake, scoop up the mixture with a ½ cup measuring cup, filling it to the rim. Then, using clean hands, form the scooped mixture into a round cake about 3 inches in diameter and ½ inch thick and set aside on the plate. Repeat with the remaining mixture, adding the cakes to the plate as you work. You should have a total of eight cakes.

Continued

Herb and Potato Fish Cakes with Lemon Caper Tartar Sauce, continued

6. *Cook the fish cakes:* Have ready a large platter. In a large skillet, heat 2 tablespoons oil over medium-high heat until shimmering. Add as many cakes to the pan in a single layer as will fit without crowding and cook, turning once, until heated through and lightly browned on both sides, about 5 minutes on each side. Transfer to the platter and keep warm. Repeat with the remaining cakes in one or two batches, wiping out the pan and heating 2 tablespoons oil before adding each new batch. Serve right away with the tartar sauce.

Notes: Make the tartar sauce up to 1 day ahead. Store in an airtight container in the fridge.

Store the uncooked fish cakes in the freezer. Arrange the cakes in a single layer in a freezer-safe airtight container. Cover with the lid and freeze. Thaw the cakes overnight in the fridge before cooking.

Cook the fish cakes up to 1 day ahead. Store in an airtight container in the fridge. To reheat, arrange them on a silicone baking sheet and drizzle the tops with olive oil. Reheat in the oven at 350°F for 15 minutes.

SERVES 

Brisket Melts with Horseradish Mayo

8 slices thick-cut brioche bread

4 tablespoons unsalted butter, at room temperature

4-ounce block sharp Cheddar cheese, shredded

16 thin slices slow-cooked brisket, about 1 pound (see page 109)

¼ cup Horseradish Mayo (recipe follows)

Yesterday's brisket is today's melty masterpiece because everything is better when sandwiched between brioche, oozing with Cheddar, and spiked with a horseradish mayo schmear!

1. *Assemble the melts (in batches, if necessary):* Heat a large cast-iron skillet or griddle pan over medium heat. Evenly spread one side of four slices of bread with 2 tablespoons of the butter. Place the slices, butter-side down, in the pan. Working quickly, top each bread slice with a generous mound (¼ cup) of cheese. Drape four brisket slices over each mound of cheese. Spread 1 tablespoon of horseradish mayo over the brisket. Close the sandwiches with the remaining four bread slices. Butter the tops evenly with the remaining 2 tablespoons butter.

2. *Cook the melts:* Cook the sandwiches until golden brown on the bottom, 4 to 5 minutes. Flip and cook until the second side is golden brown and the cheese is melted, a few minutes more. Transfer to individual plates and use a serrated knife to cut each sandwich in half. Serve now!

Horseradish Mayo

PREP UP TO 3 DAYS AHEAD

MAKES ABOUT 1 CUP

1 cup mayonnaise

2 tablespoons prepared horseradish

Use this horseradish mayo on other sandwiches, such as grilled cheese or tomato, for a spicy kick.

In a small bowl, stir together the mayo and horseradish until well combined.

Note: Store the mayo in an airtight container in the fridge.

PREP-AHEAD ELEMENT(S)

SERVES 4 TO 6

Shrimp, Burst Tomatoes, and Leek Risotto

RISOTTO

2 cups Arborio rice, rinsed and drained

3 small leeks, dark green leaves removed (see Notes, page 123), light green part finely chopped, and white part thinly sliced crosswise and reserved for the shrimp

4 garlic cloves, minced

4 cups low-sodium vegetable broth

Grated zest and juice of 1 medium lemon

1 teaspoon kosher salt

¼ teaspoon freshly ground black pepper

½ cup grated Parmigiano-Reggiano cheese

SHRIMP

1 pound fresh or thawed frozen peeled and deveined large shrimp

1 teaspoon kosher salt

Freshly ground black pepper

2 tablespoons olive oil

3 tablespoons unsalted butter, cut into small cubes

White part of leeks, reserved from risotto prep

1 cup grape tomatoes

½ teaspoon garlic powder

½ medium lemon

½ cup finely chopped fresh flat-leaf parsley for garnish

The idea of risotto as a weeknight staple is not as farfetched as you might think. By using a handy Tupperware tool, the **MICROWAVE PRESSURE COOKER**, you can cook risotto in half the time. While the pressure cooker works its magic, spend a few minutes at the stove to make a shrimp, melted leek, and burst tomato accompaniment to create a bright, creamy, luxurious dish that's impressively simple!

1. *Make the risotto:* Add the rice, light green part of the leeks, garlic, broth, lemon zest and juice, salt, and pepper to the **MICROWAVE PRESSURE COOKER** and stir to combine.

2. Lock the lid and microwave on 100 percent power for 16 minutes. At the end of the cooking time, remove the pressure cooker from the microwave and let sit to allow the pressure to release naturally, about 10 minutes. It is ready when the pressure indicator is in the down position. Only then can you lift the safety arm up and open the cover. Meanwhile, make the shrimp mixture.

3. *To make the shrimp:* Pat the shrimp dry with a clean kitchen towel and season all over with ½ teaspoon of the salt and a pinch of pepper. In a large skillet, heat the oil over high heat until shimmering. Add the shrimp in a single layer and cook, turning once, until barely pink, 30 to 45 seconds on each side. Transfer to a medium bowl and set aside.

4. Add the butter to the now-empty skillet and melt over medium-high heat. When the butter has melted, add the white part of the leeks and the tomatoes and season with the remaining ½ teaspoon salt, a pinch of pepper, and the garlic powder. Cook, stirring often, until the leeks soften and the largest tomatoes have burst, about 7 minutes.

5. Return the partially cooked shrimp to the skillet with the leeks and tomatoes and continue cooking, stirring often, until the shrimp are opaque throughout and pink

Continued

Tupperware®

Shrimp, Burst Tomatoes, and Leek Risotto, continued

all over, about 2 minutes more. Squeeze the juice from the lemon half into the pan. Using a wooden spoon, scrape up any browned bits of leek from the bottom of the pan and continue cooking, stirring continuously, for 30 seconds more. Remove from the heat.

6. When the risotto is ready, stir in the grated cheese. Divide the risotto evenly among serving dishes. Spoon the shrimp, tomatoes, and leeks over the top and garnish with the parsley. Enjoy now!

Notes: Save the leeks' dark green leaves for a homemade stock.

Make the shrimp, tomatoes, and leeks up to 2 days ahead. Store in an airtight container in the fridge. To reheat: Add 1 tablespoon of water and warm on the stovetop over low heat, stirring often, until warmed through, about 2 minutes.

Tupperware

Veggie Power

"Use the SuperSonic Choppers to finely chop veggies to sneak some extra nutrition in your family's favorite dishes."

—MARILYN B.,
33 YEARS SELLING TUPPERWARE PRODUCTS

This chapter celebrates the vibrant flavors and creativity that vegetables bring to the table. From hearty mains to standout sides—and whether you're a committed vegetarian, exploring vegan options, or just looking for delicious meat-free dishes—we've got something here for every appetite.

Roasted cabbage paired with apricot-studded lentils and a swirl of tangy harissa-infused yogurt (page 135) promises to become a cool-weather menu favorite. The flavors of charred broccoli rabe and crispy tofu draped in a spicy peanut drizzle (page 136) come together in minutes (especially when you prep the tofu ahead), while Roasted Mushroom Ragù with "Swoodles" (page 131) offers a veggie-packed dinner kids will devour—and maybe even ask for seconds! And no one will be surprised if prepping a Mediterranean Falafel Patty Platter (page 141) becomes your new "Falafel Friday."

- **ULTIMATE SILICONE STAND-UP BAGS** save fridge and freezer space. Store foods like Crispy Tofu Strips (page 128) upright or flat.
- Omit the oil and use the **MICROPRO GRILL** to cook proteins like the tofu in the Charred Broccoli Rabe and Crispy Tofu with Peanut Chili Drizzle (page 136).
- Ever cut a tomato with a dull knife? You have, and it's lousy. The **TUPPERWARE AMAZING SERIES SERRATED KNIFE** and **PARING KNIFE** are super sharp and ideal for the job of prepping tomatoes, which makes them especially helpful for recipes like Stuffed Tomatoes with Orange-Turmeric Rice and Olives (page 150).

PREP UP TO
3 DAYS AHEAD

MAKES 8 STRIPS

Crispy Tofu Strips

- One 14-ounce package firm or extra-firm tofu, drained
- 2 cups hot water
- 3 teaspoons kosher salt
- 1 cup panko bread crumbs, finely ground
- 2 teaspoons garlic powder
- 2 teaspoons smoked paprika
- 2 teaspoons ground cumin
- 3 tablespoons olive oil

These lightly breaded tofu strips combine a satisfying crunch with a soft, flavorful interior. They're delish over a kale Caesar salad (page 61) or ideal for boosting the protein in a veggie main dish, such as the charred broccoli rabe on page 136. Be sure to purchase firm or extra-firm tofu, as soft tofu will fall apart during prepping. Soaking your tofu in salt water may seem counterintuitive, but it pulls out moisture faster than pressing and gives you the firm texture needed for absorbing seasonings and marinades. Whip up these strips often and change up the spice mix, swapping turmeric for paprika or dried Italian seasoning, to make "chicken" cutlet–inspired strips (page 129).

1. Cut the tofu horizontally to make two ½-inch thick slabs. Cut each slab lengthwise into 4 strips, each about 4 inches long, 1½ inches wide, and ½ thick. In a medium bowl, combine the water and 2 teaspoons of the salt and stir until the salt dissolves. Submerge the tofu strips in the water and let soak for 15 minutes. Drain in a colander. Transfer the strips to a clean kitchen towel and pat dry.

2. *Meanwhile, make the coating:* In a medium shallow dish, stir together the panko, garlic powder, paprika, cumin, and remaining 1 teaspoon salt.

3. Add the strips to the panko mixture and turn the strips to coat thoroughly and evenly, pressing gently so the coating adheres.

4. *Cook the strips:* In a large nonstick skillet, heat the oil over medium heat until shimmering. Arrange the strips in a single layer in the pan and cook, turning once, until golden brown on both sides, 2 to 3 minutes on each side. Serve now!

Notes: For an even denser, meatier texture, freeze the tofu strips after step 1. Thaw overnight in the fridge before coating.

Store the strips in an airtight container in the fridge. Reheat in a skillet over medium heat with a splash of oil, turning occasionally, until warmed through and crisped back up, 3 to 5 minutes.

"Chicken" Cutlet and Pesto Panino Variation

Slice, stack, grill—your pesto panino is ready. Grazie, e prego! Here's how: Using a serrated knife, split a **ciabatta roll** in half horizontally. Spread **2 tablespoons pesto, homemade (page 96) or store-bought,** on the cut sides of the roll. Lay **3 Crispy Tofu Strips (page 128)** on the roll bottom and top with **2 mozzarella cheese slices, 1 beefsteak tomato slice,** and **a few arugula leaves.** Close with the roll top, pesto-side down. Brush the outside of the roll with **olive oil.** Heat a stovetop grill pan over medium-high heat. Place the panino in the hot pan and press down firmly with a spatula. Grill until golden on the underside, about 3 minutes. Flip the panino, press down with the spatula, and grill until golden on the second side and the cheese is melted, about 3 minutes more. Transfer to a plate, let cool slightly, cut in half, and enjoy.

PREP-AHEAD ELEMENT(S)

SERVES 4 TO 6

Roasted Mushroom Ragù with "Swoodles"

MUSHROOM RAGÙ

1½ pounds mushrooms (such as button or cremini), woody stems trimmed and caps halved

3 tablespoons olive oil

Leaves from 10 thyme sprigs

1 teaspoon kosher salt

½ teaspoon freshly ground black pepper

1 small yellow onion, finely diced

2 garlic cloves, minced

2 tablespoons tomato paste

1 medium carrot, peeled and grated

One 14-ounce can crushed tomatoes

2 cups low-sodium vegetable broth

SWOODLES

2 medium sweet potatoes, peeled and spiralized

½ teaspoon kosher salt

2 tablespoons olive oil, plus more if needed

Grated Parmigiano-Reggiano or vegan Parmesan-style cheese for garnish

Meet "swoodles"—sweet potato noodles. They're easy to make with a spiralizer. Kids will love turning the handle, and unofficial "parent" data says that when kids help in the kitchen, they're more likely (🤞) to eat the sweet potatoes, giving you another nutritious carb to serve that looks just like their favorite, pasta. Use the spiralizer to transform carrots, parsnips, zucchini, and cucumbers into spaghetti-like ribbons too. The comforting mushroom ragù—a vegan riff on Bolognese meat sauce—is rich and loaded with onion, carrots, and tomatoes.

1. Preheat the oven to 400°F. Line a metal sheet pan with a silicone baking sheet.

2. *Prep the mushrooms:* In a large bowl, toss the mushrooms with 2 tablespoons of the oil, the thyme, ½ teaspoon of the salt, and ¼ teaspoon of the pepper. Arrange the mushrooms in a single layer on the prepared sheet pan. Roast until the mushrooms are deeply browned, about 20 minutes. Remove from the oven and let cool for 10 minutes. Transfer to a food processor and pulse until the mushrooms are finely chopped. Set aside.

3. In a medium saucepan or Dutch oven, heat the remaining 1 tablespoon oil over medium heat until shimmering. Add the onion and cook, stirring often, until lightly golden, about 3 minutes. Add the garlic and cook, stirring often, until fragrant, about 1 minute. Add the tomato paste and cook, stirring, until the color darkens, about 1 minute more.

4. Add the carrot and the remaining ½ teaspoon salt and ¼ teaspoon pepper and cook, stirring, until the carrot softens slightly, about 3 minutes. Add the mushrooms, crushed tomatoes, and broth and bring to a boil. Turn down the heat to low and simmer uncovered, stirring now and then, until the liquid reduces slightly, 15 to 20 minutes.

5. *Make the swoodles:* Have ready a large bowl. Sprinkle the sweet potatoes with salt and gently toss to season.

Continued

Roasted Mushroom Ragù with "Swoodles," continued

In a large skillet, heat the oil over medium heat until shimmering. Working in batches to avoid crowding, add the sweet potatoes and cook, tossing frequently, until slightly softened, 2 to 3 minutes. Transfer to the bowl and keep warm. Repeat with the remaining sweet potatoes, adding more oil to the pan if needed to prevent sticking. Season the swoodles with salt.

6. *To serve:* Divide the swoodles among individual bowls. Top with generous spoonfuls of the ragù and toss gently to coat. Garnish with the cheese and serve right away.

Note: Make the mushroom ragù up to 3 days ahead. While you're at it, prep a double batch of mushrooms in step 2. Use the extra batch for serving over toast or adding to omelets. Reheat the ragù in a saucepan over medium-low heat, stirring occasionally, until heated through, 5 to 10 minutes. Add a splash of water or broth and continue heating if it's too thick.

Polenta Variation

Switch up this dish by serving the mushroom ragù over creamy, stick-to-your-ribs polenta. Here's how to cook and serve the polenta: Preheat the oven to 350°F. In a 2-quart baking dish, stir together **1 cup polenta** and **4 cups vegetable broth** and season with **1 teaspoon kosher salt**. Cover and bake, stirring halfway through the cooking time, until tender and creamy, about 40 minutes. Divide the polenta among individual bowls and garnish with grated Parmigiano-Reggiano cheese, if you like. Spoon the ragù over the polenta, then top with more cheese.

Lighten your meal prep by cooking the polenta in the oven up to 3 days ahead, then let cool and store in the fridge. To reheat: In a medium saucepan over low heat, add the polenta, breaking it up with a wooden spoon if needed, and a few splashes of broth. Whisk to smooth out any lumps and restore a creamy consistency then bake as directed.

PREP UP TO
2 DAYS AHEAD

SERVES 4

Roasted Cabbage, Apricot Lentils, and Harissa Yogurt

CABBAGE

1 small head green cabbage (about 1 pound), core intact (it holds the leaves together), cut through the stem end into 8 wedges

Olive oil for drizzling

1½ teaspoons kosher salt

½ teaspoon freshly ground black pepper

1½ teaspoons ground coriander

LENTILS

1 cup green lentils

2 cups low-sodium vegetable broth, plus more if needed

Kosher salt

10 to 12 dried apricots, roughly chopped

HARISSA YOGURT

1 cup plain full-fat Greek yogurt

1 teaspoon harissa paste, plus more if needed

Pinch of kosher salt

Juice of ½ lemon

In this dish, coriander-spiced cabbage wedges crisp up gloriously in a hot oven, and a hearty helping of lentils keeps everyone satisfied. The apricots in the lentils and the harissa in the yogurt combine to deliver a perfect sweet-and-spicy pairing.

1. Preheat the oven to 400°F. Line a metal sheet pan with a silicone baking sheet.

2. *Make the cabbage:* Arrange the cabbage wedges in a single layer on the prepared sheet pan. Drizzle with oil and season with the salt, pepper, and coriander on both sides. Roast the wedges, flipping once halfway through the cooking time, until the core of each cabbage wedge is tender and some of the leaves are charred black, about 40 minutes.

3. *Meanwhile, make the lentils:* In a small saucepan with a tight-fitting lid, combine the lentils with the broth to cover by 2 inches. Bring to a boil over high heat, turn down the heat to low, cover, and cook until the lentils are tender and the water is absorbed, 12 to 15 minutes. Remove from the heat and season to taste with salt. Stir in ½ cup of the apricots and set aside.

4. *Make the harissa yogurt:* In a small bowl, stir together the yogurt, harissa, salt, and lemon juice. Taste and add more harissa, if desired.

5. *To serve:* Divide the apricot lentils evenly among individual plates and top each serving with two cabbage wedges. Drizzle some of the harissa yogurt over the top and garnish with the remaining apricots. Serve at once with the remaining yogurt alongside.

Notes: Store the harissa yogurt in an airtight container in the fridge. Before serving, stir it to see if it has thickened too much. If it has, stir in lemon juice until thinned to a good drizzling consistency.

Store the cabbage and lentils in separate airtight containers in the fridge. To reheat the cabbage: Microwave with a splash of water at 50 percent power until warmed through, about 5 minutes, flipping halfway through. To reheat the lentils: In a saucepan over low heat, warm the lentil mixture and a splash of water, stirring frequently until heated through, about 4 minutes.

PREP-AHEAD ELEMENT(S)

SERVES 4

Charred Broccoli Rabe and Crispy Tofu with Peanut Chili Drizzle

Crispy tofu paired with charred broccoli rabe and spicy peanut drizzle is pure magic—the perfect balance of crunch, bitterness, and dual punches of sweetness and heat. Make it on repeat: store bunches of unwashed broccoli rabe in airtight containers in the fridge to keep them fresher longer.

BROCCOLI RABE

2 bunches broccoli rabe (about 2 pounds), tough ends trimmed and tender stems and leaves coarsely chopped

3 tablespoons olive oil

1 teaspoon kosher salt

2 garlic cloves, minced

PEANUT CHILI DRIZZLE

¼ cup creamy peanut butter

2 tablespoons soy sauce

Grated zest of 1 lime

2 teaspoons chili crisp

1 tablespoon extra-virgin olive oil

4 tablespoons water

8 Crispy Tofu Strips (page 128)

¼ cup crushed salted roasted peanuts for garnish

Grated zest of 1 lime for garnish

1. Preheat the oven to 375°F. Line a metal sheet pan with a silicone baking sheet.

2. *Make the broccoli rabe:* Put the broccoli rabe in a large bowl. Add the oil, salt, and garlic and toss to coat evenly.

3. Arrange the broccoli rabe in a single layer on the prepared sheet pan. Roast until wilted, about 10 minutes. Use tongs to toss and then continue roasting until the leaves are crisp and the stems are fork-tender, about 7 minutes more.

4. *Meanwhile, make the peanut chili drizzle:* In a small bowl, whisk together the peanut butter, soy sauce, lime juice, chili crisp, and oil until smooth. Slowly whisk in the water, 1 tablespoon at a time, to thin to a good drizzling consistency. Set aside.

5. *To serve:* Arrange the broccoli rabe on a platter. Top with the tofu strips and the peanut drizzle, then garnish with the peanuts and lime zest. Serve right away.

Note: Make the broccoli rabe up to 2 days ahead. Store in an airtight container in the fridge.

PREP UP TO
2 DAYS AHEAD

SERVES 4

Maple-Glazed Acorn Squash and Tempeh with Pomegranate Arils

Think of tempeh as tofu's hearty cousin—fermented soy with a nutty, earthy flavor, a firm texture, and loads of protein and fiber. A quick simmer removes any bitterness and allows this traditional Indonesian soy product to absorb the flavors of the glaze. This vegan main course is satisfying and full of flavor: the sweet-glazed squash enhances tempeh's savory bite, while the pomegranate arils add a burst of tartness and color and the pumpkin seeds deliver a welcome crunch. Hosting vegan friends? This dish is it.

TEMPEH

Two 8-ounce packages tempeh

2 tablespoons olive oil

Kosher salt and freshly ground black pepper

2 tablespoons cornstarch

MAPLE GLAZE

½ cup maple syrup

2 tablespoons soy sauce

2 tablespoons sriracha or other hot sauce

2 tablespoons ginger paste

1 tablespoon fresh lime juice

SQUASH

1 large or 2 small acorn squashes (2 pounds), halved lengthwise, seeded, and cut crosswise into ½-inch-thick slices (see Notes, page 140)

2 tablespoons olive oil

1 teaspoon kosher salt

¼ teaspoon freshly ground black pepper

Toasted pumpkin seeds for garnish

½ cup pomegranate arils or dried cranberries for garnish

1. Preheat the oven to 400°F. Line a large metal sheet pan with a silicone baking sheet.

2. *Prep the tempeh:* In a large skillet, combine the tempeh with water to cover and bring to a boil over high heat. Turn down the heat to a simmer and cook for 8 minutes. Remove from the heat.

3. Transfer the tempeh to a cutting board, pat dry with a clean kitchen towel, and cut into 1-inch cubes. Transfer the cubes to a medium bowl, drizzle with the oil, season generously with salt and pepper, and toss to coat evenly. Add the cornstarch and toss again until each cube is thoroughly and evenly coated. Arrange the tempeh cubes in a single layer on half of the prepared sheet pan.

4. *Make the maple glaze:* In a small bowl, whisk together the maple syrup, soy sauce, hot sauce, ginger, and lime juice.

5. *Prep the squash:* Put the squash slices in a medium bowl, drizzle with the oil, season with the salt and pepper, and toss to coat evenly. Pour half of the maple glaze over the squash pieces and toss to coat evenly. Arrange the squash pieces in a single layer on the empty half of the prepared sheet pan. Drizzle the remaining maple glaze over the tempeh pieces.

6. Roast the tempeh and squash, turning them halfway through the cooking time, until the tempeh is crispy, the squash is tender, and both show signs of glazed sticky goodness, 25 to 30 minutes.

Continued

Maple-Glazed Acorn Squash and Tempeh with Pomegranate Arils, continued

7. *To serve:* Arrange the squash slices and tempeh on a serving platter and scatter the pumpkin seeds and pomegranate arils across the top. Serve now.

Notes: Microwave the squash at 100 percent power for 5 minutes to soften the skin to make it easier to slice.

Make the dish up to 2 days ahead, omitting the pumpkin seeds and pomegranate arils. Store in an airtight container in the fridge. To reheat: Microwave the squash and tempeh at 50 percent power until warmed through, about 2 minutes, flipping halfway through the reheating time. Garnish with the pumpkin seeds and pomegranate arils before serving.

Mediterranean Falafel Patty Platter

SERVES 6

These herby, aromatic chickpea falafel patties burst with fiber and protein and are a prep-ahead powerhouse! Tuck them into your kids' lunch boxes with fresh veggies, hummus, or tzatziki dressing (see page 65) for dipping, build a pita sandwich, or go big and create a bold, vibrant platter for sharing.

BASE

16 cooked falafel patties (plan on 2 or 3 patties per person; recipe follows)

PLATTER SUGGESTIONS

Assorted fresh or quick pickled vegetables (page 79) of choice (such as red onions and radishes)

Baba Ghanoush (recipe follows)

Halved cherry tomatoes

Cucumber slices

Crumbled feta cheese

Stuffed grape leaves (dolmas)

Hummus

Grilled Green Onions (recipe follows) or other grilled vegetables (such as zucchini, bell peppers, or asparagus)

Kalamata olives or other black, green, or assorted olives

Pita bread, cut into triangles and toasted for dipping or halved crosswise for sandwiches

Tahini Sauce (recipe follows)

Tzatziki dressing (see page 65)

HOW TO SET UP

- Get ahead by prepping the falafel mixture and preferred sides in advance.
- Set out a large serving platter with colorful serving bowls of sauce, dip, and/or vegetables and pita.
- Bake or fry the falafel patties. Serve hot and paired as you wish, such as drizzled with Tahini Sauce and topped with Grilled Green Onions, cherry tomatoes, and feta cheese. Or build a sandwich!

PREP UP TO 1 DAY AHEAD

MAKES 16 PATTIES

4 cups dried chickpeas

½ teaspoon baking soda

Small handful of fresh flat-leaf parsley leaves, roughly chopped

1 small red onion, roughly chopped

2 tablespoons kosher salt, plus more for finishing

2 tablespoons ground cumin

2 tablespoons garlic powder

2 tablespoons smoked paprika

1 tablespoon chickpea flour (see Note, page 146)

Olive oil for cooking

Falafel Patties

Soaking dried chickpeas overnight will give you the best falafel mixture for making compact patties that you can bake or fry to crispy on the outside and tender on the inside.

1. *One day in advance, prep the chickpeas:* Put the chickpeas into a large bowl, add water to cover by 3 inches and the baking soda, and stir to combine. Cover and let soak on the counter overnight.

2. The next day, drain the chickpeas. Lay a large, clean kitchen towel on the counter. Transfer the chickpeas to the towel and pat to dry thoroughly.

3. *Make the falafel mixture:* Transfer the chickpeas, parsley, onion, salt, cumin, garlic powder, and paprika to a food processor. Pulse, stopping now and then to scrape down the sides of the bowl, until the mixture resembles wet sand. To test, squeeze a little of the mixture in your hand; if it holds together, it's ready. If not, pulse a few more times.

4. Transfer the mixture to a large bowl. Using a silicone spatula, stir in the chickpea flour until thoroughly combined and the texture of the mixture goes from wet sand to a thick paste. It will stick to the sides of the bowl. Cover and refrigerate for 30 minutes.

5. *Form and cook the falafel patties:* Line a metal sheet pan with a silicone baking sheet. Scoop about ¼ cup of the mixture onto the prepared sheet to form a round, flat patty. You should have sixteen patties, each 3 inches in diameter and ½ inch thick. If baking the patties, preheat the oven to 350°F. If frying the patties, have ready a large skillet.

6. *Cook the patties:* If baking the patties, drizzle them lightly with oil. Bake, flipping them halfway through the cooking time, until browned and crispy, 18 to 20 minutes. If frying the patties, have ready a large plate. In a large nonstick skillet, heat 2 tablespoons oil over medium heat until shimmering. Add as many patties to the pan in a single layer as will fit without crowding and cook until crispy and browned on the bottom, 2 to 3 minutes. Flip and cook until crispy and browned on the second side, 2 to 3 minutes more. Transfer to the plate. Repeat with the remaining patties in one

Continued

Falafel Patties, continued

or two batches as needed, wiping out the pan and heating 2 tablespoons oil before adding a new batch. Serve hot, sprinkled with more salt to taste, and enjoy as you wish.

Note: Chickpea or garbanzo bean flour is a fine, pale-yellow, gluten-free flour made by finely grinding dried chickpeas. It helps bind the mixture and adds nutty flavor without adding extra moisture.

Tahini Sauce

PREP UP TO 2 DAYS AHEAD

MAKES ABOUT ¾ CUP

- ½ cup tahini
- Juice of 1 lemon
- 2 garlic cloves, minced
- ¼ teaspoon kosher salt
- ¼ teaspoon smoked paprika
- ¼ cup plus 2 tablespoons water

Drizzle this easy-to-make sauce over falafel patties for a lemony, nutty, garlicky lift.

In a small bowl, whisk together the tahini, lemon juice, garlic, salt, and paprika until smooth and thick. Slowly whisk in the ¼ cup of the water, then add the remaining 2 tablespoons, 1 tablespoon at a time, until the sauce is smooth and pourable. Taste and adjust the seasoning with salt if needed.

Note: Store the tahini sauce in an airtight container in the fridge. Whisk in a squeeze of fresh lemon juice or a little water to thin to desired consistency before serving.

Grilled Green Onions

SERVES 6

- 2 to 3 bunches green onions, green and white parts, root ends trimmed
- 1 tablespoon olive oil
- ½ teaspoon smoked paprika
- Kosher salt

Green onions impart a subtle sweetness to crispy falafel patties and nicely contrast with bolder pickled veggies.

1. Put the green onions in a shallow medium bowl. Drizzle with oil, sprinkle with the paprika, season with salt, and toss to coat evenly.

2. Heat a grill pan over medium-high heat. Arrange the green onions in a single layer on the hot pan and cook, flipping once halfway through the cooking time, until charred and tender on both sides, 2 to 3 minutes on each side. Serve right away.

PREP UP TO 2 DAYS AHEAD
MAKES ABOUT 2 CUPS

1 pound eggplant, cut into 1-inch cubes

Kosher salt

Extra-virgin olive oil for drizzling

½ cup tahini

2 teaspoons ground cumin

Juice of 1 lemon

Sesame seeds for garnish

Pomegranate arils for garnish (optional)

Baba Ghanoush

Dip warm pita in this creamy roasted eggplant dip or slather it on a falafel patty. Pomegranate arils add a tart pop of flavor and bright color.

1. Preheat the oven to 425°F. Line a metal sheet pan with a silicone baking sheet.

2. *Cook the eggplant:* Put the eggplant cubes on the prepared sheet pan. Season with salt, drizzle with oil, and toss to coat evenly. Spread in a single layer. Roast until the eggplant is soft and golden in spots, 25 to 30 minutes. Remove from the oven and let cool completely, about 30 minutes.

3. *Make the dip:* In a food processor, combine the eggplant, tahini, 2 teaspoons salt, the cumin, and lemon juice and pulse until smooth.

4. Transfer the dip to a serving bowl or shallow serving dish. Drizzle with oil, sprinkle with sesame seeds and pomegranate arils (if using), and sprinkle with salt.

Note: Store the baba ghanoush in an airtight container in the fridge. For the best flavor, bring to room temperature before serving.

PREP UP TO
2 DAYS AHEAD

SERVES 4

Walnut, Feta, and Herb Zucchini Boats

4 medium zucchini

Kosher salt and freshly ground black pepper

2 tablespoons olive oil, plus more for drizzling

1 small yellow onion, finely diced

2 garlic cloves, minced

½ cup finely chopped walnuts

2 tablespoons soy sauce

½ cup panko bread crumbs

¼ cup finely chopped mixed fresh herbs (such as dill, flat-leaf parsley, and mint), plus more for garnish

½ cup crumbled feta cheese

Lemon wedges for serving

Walnuts are rich in heart-healthy fats and packed with umami flavor. When finely chopped and mixed with panko and fresh herbs, they create a new way to enjoy "meaty" stuffed zucchini boats. The texture mimics a traditional sausage filling, making this easy vegetarian recipe a weeknight winner.

1. Preheat the oven to 350°F. Line a metal sheet pan with a silicone baking sheet.

2. *Prep the zucchini:* Have ready a small bowl. Cut each zucchini in half lengthwise. Using a small spoon, scoop out the flesh, leaving a ¼-inch-thick shell, and add the flesh to the bowl. Arrange the zucchini boats, hollow-side up, on the prepared sheet pan. Season the hollows with salt and pepper.

3. *Make the filling:* In a medium skillet, warm the oil over medium heat until shimmering. Add the onion and cook, stirring often, until lightly golden, about 3 minutes. Add the garlic and cook, stirring often, until fragrant, about 30 seconds. Add the reserved zucchini flesh, season with 1 teaspoon salt and with pepper to taste, and cook, stirring often, until the zucchini softens and most of the water in the pan has evaporated, about 5 minutes. Stir in the walnuts and soy sauce and cook, stirring, for 30 seconds more. Remove from the heat. Stir in the panko and herbs, mixing well.

4. *Stuff and bake the zucchini:* Fill each zucchini shell with 3 to 4 tablespoons of the filling, packing it lightly. Scatter the feta evenly across the tops, then drizzle with oil. Bake until the zucchini shells are tender and the tops are golden, 30 to 35 minutes.

5. Serve now, garnished with more herbs and with lemon wedges on the side.

Note: Store the boats in an airtight container in the fridge. Reheat uncovered in the oven at 350°F until warmed through, about 15 minutes.

PREP UP TO
1 DAY AHEAD

SERVES 6 AS A SIDE DISH, 3 AS A MAIN COURSE

Stuffed Tomatoes with Orange-Turmeric Rice and Olives

6 large, firm beefsteak tomatoes

Kosher salt and freshly ground black pepper

2 tablespoons olive oil, plus more for drizzling

1 small red onion, finely diced

1 tablespoon ground turmeric

½ cup jasmine rice

¾ cup pitted Castelvetrano or other green olives, crushed

1 cup packed baby spinach leaves

Zest and juice of 1 orange

1 large zucchini, ends trimmed, halved crosswise then halved lengthwise

Here, beefsteak tomatoes are stuffed with flavor-packed turmeric rice that has notes of sweet citrus, earthy spinach, and buttery, briny olive. The zucchini roasts along with the tomatoes and turns out to be a velvety, sweet veggie bonus.

1. Preheat the oven to 400°F.

2. Set a fine-mesh strainer over a bowl. Using a serrated knife, cut a slice off the top of each tomato and reserve. Using a paring knife, carefully slice around the core of each tomato, lift out, and discard. Using a pointed spoon, scrape and scoop out the pulp and seeds from each tomato, being careful not to pierce the walls or bottom, and transfer to the strainer. Reserve the juice and pulp; discard the seeds.

3. In a medium skillet, heat 1 tablespoon of the oil over medium heat until shimmering. Add the onion and cook, stirring often, until soft, about 5 minutes. Stir in the remaining 1 tablespoon oil and the turmeric and continue cooking, stirring, about 30 seconds. Add the rice and toast, stirring often, until fragrant, about 1 minute. Add the reserved tomato pulp and juices, olives, spinach, and orange zest and juice and cook, stirring often, until the spinach wilts, about 30 seconds more.

4. Arrange the tomatoes, hollow-side up, in a 9 by 13-inch baking dish with a cover. Generously season the insides with salt. Divide the rice mixture evenly among the tomatoes, filling them almost to the top and packing the mixture in with a spoon. Place the tops on the tomatoes.

5. Drizzle the zucchini with oil, season generously with salt and pepper, and toss to coat. Tuck the zucchini among the tomatoes to stabilize them.

6. Pour 2 cups of water into the bottom of the baking dish. Cover and bake until the tomatoes are soft and beginning to collapse and the rice stuffing is cooked, about 1 hour. Let cool slightly and serve.

Note: Store the stuffed, uncooked tomatoes covered in the fridge until ready to bake.

PREP UP TO
2 DAYS AHEAD

SERVES 4 TO 6

Cauliflower with Couscous and Salsa Verde

SALSA VERDE

¼ cup extra-virgin olive oil

2 tablespoons red wine vinegar

Leaves and tender stems from 1 small bunch flat-leaf parsley

2 garlic cloves

2 teaspoons Dijon mustard

2 tablespoons medium capers packed in salt, well rinsed, or in brine, drained

CAULIFLOWER

1 large head cauliflower (about 1 pound), cored, broken into bite-size florets, and leaves reserved

1 large red onion, quartered, core discarded, and petaled (see headnote)

2 tablespoons olive oil

1 teaspoon kosher salt

1 teaspoon smoked paprika

1 teaspoon ground cumin

COUSCOUS

1½ cups water

1½ teaspoons kosher salt

1 cup pearl couscous

½ cup golden raisins or dried cranberries

Here, sheet pan–roasted cauliflower and red onion sit atop a bed of pearl couscous tossed with golden raisins and salsa verde for a vegan dish with lots of big flavor. This recipe requires a little extra technique, but it's worth it: to "petal" a red onion means to separate a quartered onion into its natural curved layers, which resemble flower petals. This helps them cook more evenly. Make sure you're using a razor-sharp knife for clean cuts, resulting in less tears during onion prep—yes, you cry because your knife is dull.

1. Preheat the oven to 425°F. Line a metal sheet pan with a silicone baking sheet.

2. *Make the salsa verde:* In a food processor, combine the oil, vinegar, parsley, garlic, mustard, and capers and pulse 3 or 4 times until the parsley stems are well chopped but the sauce still has texture. Set aside until ready to use.

3. *Make the cauliflower:* Put the cauliflower florets and leaves (yes, eat them—they're good!) and red onion in a large bowl. Add the oil, salt, paprika, and cumin and toss to coat evenly. Spread the mixture on the prepared sheet pan. Roast until the cauliflower florets and onion are tender and golden and the cauliflower leaves are crispy, 25 to 30 minutes.

4. *Meanwhile, make the couscous:* Bring the water to a boil in a small saucepan with a tight-fitting lid. Add the salt and couscous to the boiling water, turn down the heat to low, cover, and cook until the couscous is tender and all the liquid is absorbed, 12 to 14 minutes. Remove from the heat and transfer to a medium bowl. Stir in the raisins and a heaping spoonful of the reserved salsa verde.

5. *To serve:* Arrange the couscous in a bed on a serving platter. Scatter the roasted cauliflower florets and leaves and onion petals over the couscous and top with spoonfuls of the salsa verde.

Note: Store the dish in an airtight container in the fridge. Enjoy cold, or reheat in the microwave on 50-percent power until warmed through, about 2 minutes. Fluff with a fork before serving.

Happy Kids, Happy Planet

"I've learned ways to conserve the environment, make food last longer, maintain freshness. I have learned that my children are far more independent with preparing food because of the ease of using Tupperware. My eight-year-olds can do their own eggs, pop their own popcorn, and so much more."

—CARRIE R.,
10 YEARS SELLING TUPPERWARE PRODUCTS

Cooking for—and with—kids is about creating memories, sparking creativity, and teaching little hands how to care for themselves, their families, and the world around them.

In this chapter, the recipes were developed with easy prep tasks for kids in mind. From helping to make scrumptious Lasagna Rolls with Pork Ragù (page 159) to folding veggie wonton triangles (page 165) and scooping and dropping coconut macaroons (page 194) onto a sheet pan, every dish offers a chance for kids to learn about prepping and cooking meals and treats from scratch and how, as a family, you make sustainable choices by reducing food waste and the use of single-use plastics, aluminum foil, parchment paper, and throwaway containers.

Kids will be so happy to make (and eat!) these dishes with you.

- **THATSA BOWL** has a generous, roomy size for all-in-one mixing and kneading, making easy prep work for pizzas, like the Mini Deep-Dish Pizzas (page 185).
- When little tummies start to rumble, **SUPERSONIC CHOPPERS** make whipping up Afternoon Spreads (page 182) quick and easy—just right for pairing with crackers, veggie sticks, or pita chips.
- The **GRATE 'N STORE** grates pecorino romano finely or coarsely and doubles as a storage container, so you have fresh cheese at the ready for mixing or sprinkling on your Lasagna Rolls with Pork Ragù (page 159).
- Use the **SMART MULTI-COOKER** for making soups, like the Quick Wonton Soup on page 166.

PREP UP TO
2 DAYS AHEAD

FREEZER-FRIENDLY
UP TO 3 MONTHS

SERVES 4 TO 6

Lasagna Rolls with Pork Ragù

Lasagna rolls bring all the comfort of a classic lasagna but in an easier-to-serve kid-friendly format. Pack the rolls with meat sauce and cheesy layers or swap the meat ragù for mushroom ragù (page 131) for a veggie version. Kids can get involved by grating the cheese, spooning the filling, and rolling up the noodles.

RAGÙ

1 tablespoon olive oil

1 tablespoon unsalted butter

1 small yellow onion, finely diced

1 cup shredded carrot (from about 2 medium carrots)

2 garlic cloves, minced

1 pound ground pork

2 teaspoons kosher salt

¼ teaspoon freshly ground black pepper

One 28-ounce can crushed tomatoes

1 cup low-sodium chicken broth

2 tablespoons grated pecorino romano cheese

LASAGNA

12 lasagna noodles

One 15-ounce container whole-milk ricotta cheese

¼ cup grated pecorino romano cheese

1¼ cup shredded mozzarella cheese

½ teaspoon garlic powder

¼ cup finely chopped fresh flat-leaf parsley

1 egg, lightly beaten

1. *Make the ragù:* In a medium saucepan or Dutch oven with a lid, heat the olive oil and butter over medium heat until the butter melts. Add the onion and carrot and cook, stirring often, until the vegetables soften, 3 to 5 minutes. Add garlic and cook, stirring often, until fragrant, about 1 minute more. Add the pork, season with the salt and pepper, and cook, stirring and breaking up the pork with the back of a wooden spoon, until browned, about 4 minutes.

2. Stir in the tomatoes and broth, cover with the lid ajar, turn down the heat to low, and cook, stirring occasionally, until the sauce thickens and pork is cooked through, about 30 minutes. Stir in the pecorino and remove from the heat. Let cool for 15 minutes.

3. *Meanwhile, cook the noodles and make the filling:* Bring a large pot of generously salted water to boil. Add the lasagna noodles and cook according to the directions on the package for 1 minute less than al dente. Drain into a colander and rinse under cold running water to stop the cooking. Lay the noodles in a single layer on a large cutting board. Preheat the oven to 350°F.

4. In a medium bowl, stir together the ricotta, pecorino, ¼ cup of the mozzarella, the garlic powder, parsley, and egg until smooth.

5. *Fill and roll the noodles:* Spread about 3 tablespoons of the ricotta mixture in a thin layer the length of each noodle. Spoon about 2 tablespoons of the ragù evenly over the ricotta. Starting at a narrow end, gently roll up a noodle and set aside seam-side down. Repeat with the remaining filling and noodles.

Continued

Lasagna Rolls with Pork Ragù, continued

6. In the bottom of a 9 by 13-inch lasagna or baking dish, spread 1 cup of the ragù. Arrange the lasagna rolls, seam-side down and side by side, in the dish, creating three rows of four rolls each. Top with the remaining ragù. Scatter the remaining 1 cup mozzarella evenly over the top.

7. *Bake and serve:* Cover the dish and bake until the cheese on top is browned and bubbly and the noodles are tender, about 40 minutes. Let rest for 10 minutes before serving.

Note: Store the dish covered in the fridge. Reheat covered in the oven at 350°F until warmed through, 25 to 30 minutes. To freeze for later, assemble the rolls but do not bake. Bake, covered, directly from the freezer in the oven at 375°F for about 1 hour.

Popcorn Party

PREP UP TO 1 WEEK AHEAD

MAKES SEASONING FOR 5 TO 6 CUPS OF POPCORN

Popcorn is great, but buttered and seasoned popcorn is next level. That's especially true when you have a microwave popcorn maker on hand like the TUPPERWARE WOW POP MICROWAVE POPCORN MAKER, which translates to less waste, easy prep, and delicious results!

Here's how to put your popcorn maker to work, plus three seasonings.

Fall Mix

½ cup finely chopped dried apple rings

3 tablespoons pumpkin pie spice

2 tablespoons light brown sugar

1 teaspoon kosher salt

In a small bowl, stir together the apple rings, pumpkin pie spice, brown sugar, and salt.

Dill Pickle and Seaweed

2 nori sheets, each about 7 by 8 inches, finely crushed

3 tablespoons dried dill

1 teaspoon kosher salt

½ teaspoon garlic powder

Pinch of mustard powder

In a small bowl, stir together the nori, dill, salt, garlic powder, and mustard powder.

Nacho Cheese

½ cup nutritional yeast

1 teaspoon garlic powder

1 teaspoon onion powder

1 teaspoon smoked paprika

1 teaspoon kosher salt

½ teaspoon ground cumin

In a small bowl, stir together the nutritional yeast, garlic powder, onion powder, paprika, salt, and cumin.

---

1. Prepare your choice of seasoning mix (recipes at left.)

2. Pop ¼ cup kernels into the microwave popcorn maker according to the manufacturer's instructions. If using the **WOW POP** popper, position the lid in *vent* position and follow Tupperware instructions.

3. Open the popcorn maker and add 2 tablespoons unsalted butter, at room temperature, and the seasoning mix. If using the **WOW POP** popper, re-cover with the lid in *shake* position. Vigorously shake to season the popcorn evenly. Open the lid and eat!

FREEZER-FRIENDLY
UP TO 3 MONTHS

MAKES ABOUT 30 TRIANGLES

Veggie Wonton Triangles with Sesame Dipping Sauce

WONTON TRIANGLES

2 teaspoons toasted sesame oil, plus more for brushing

2 cups finely shredded napa cabbage (about ¼ medium head)

2 green onions, light green and white parts, finely chopped

2 garlic cloves, minced

8 ounces button mushrooms, tough stems trimmed and caps pulsed in a food processor until finely ground (about 2 cups)

1 tablespoon white miso paste

4 ounces extra-firm tofu, finely chopped

2 tablespoons soy sauce

1 teaspoon rice vinegar

30 wonton wrappers, at room temperature

DIPPING SAUCE

½ cup soy sauce

2 tablespoons rice vinegar

2 teaspoons toasted sesame oil

2 teaspoons honey

2 teaspoons finely chopped green onion, light green and white parts

Sesame seeds for garnish

Finely chopped green onions, dark green parts only, for garnish

These protein-packed wonton triangles are the ultimate kid-approved snack-meal hybrid. Their small, triangular shape makes them easy to grab, dip, and devour without a mess. Making these is a simple, hands-on kitchen project that kids can easily do alongside you. Double the recipe and freeze half for later.

1. *Prep the filling:* In a large nonstick skillet, heat the oil over medium heat until shimmering. Add the cabbage, green onions, and garlic and cook, stirring often, until the cabbage softens, about 3 minutes. Add the mushrooms and miso paste and continue cooking, stirring occasionally, until the mushrooms release their liquid, about 4 minutes more. Stir in the tofu, soy sauce, and vinegar and continue cooking, stirring often, until the liquid in the pan mostly evaporates, 5 to 7 minutes more. Transfer the mixture to a medium bowl and let cool for 15 minutes.

2. Preheat the oven to 400°F. Line a metal sheet pan with a silicone baking sheet.

3. *Fill and fold the triangles:* Fill a small bowl with water and set it near a large, clean work surface. Place a wonton wrapper on the work surface. Scoop up 1 tablespoon of the filling and place slightly off-center on the wrapper. Dip your finger or a pastry brush into the bowl of water and trace the edges of the wrapper. Fold the wrapper in half over the filling to form a triangle. Press the edges firmly to seal and place the triangle on the prepared sheet pan. Repeat filling, folding, and sealing the remaining wrappers. You should have about thirty triangles.

4. *Bake the triangles:* Lightly brush the tops of the triangles with sesame oil. Bake the triangles, flipping them halfway through the cooking time, until golden brown and crispy, 10 to 12 minutes.

Continued

Veggie Wonton Triangles with Sesame Dipping Sauce, continued

5. *Meanwhile, make the dipping sauce:* In a small bowl, whisk together the soy sauce, vinegar, oil, honey, and green onion. Sprinkle the sesame seeds over the top.

6. Transfer the triangles to a serving platter and garnish with the green onion. Serve right away, with the sauce alongside for dipping.

Note: Freeze unbaked, assembled wonton triangles uncovered on a sheet pan until firm, about 2 hours, then transfer to an airtight container and return to the freezer. Bake directly from the freezer, adding 2 to 3 minutes to the directed cooking time.

Quick Wonton Soup Variation

Spin frozen veggie wonton triangles into an entirely new meal that serves two. Pour **4 cups broth (such as miso, vegetable, or chicken)** into a medium saucepan and bring to a boil over high heat. Add **8 frozen veggie wonton triangles** and **1 cup finely chopped baby bok choy.** Turn down the heat to a gentle simmer and cook until the wontons float to the top, about 5 minutes. Divide the broth, wontons, and bok choy evenly between two bowls and drizzle with **soy sauce to taste.** Garnish with **sliced green onions** and **sesame seeds** and enjoy.

PREP-AHEAD ELEMENT(S)

SERVES 6 TO 8

Brisket Stroganoff

Brisket stroganoff may sound like a lot of work, but most of the effort is already done with prep-ahead Slow-Cooked Brisket and Onions (page 109). From there, it's as simple as stirring in creamy sour cream and a quick mushroom sauce, then popping the whole shebang into the oven. This dish is hearty, cozy, beefy noodle comfort food that's perfect for cold days. Save space in the fridge by storing leftovers in reusable stand-up silicone bags, then reheat in the microwave with the bag partially opened for lunch the next day.

NOODLES

Two 12-ounce packages dried extra-wide egg noodles

1 pound brisket, shredded (from Slow-Cooked Brisket and Onions, page 109)

2 cups full-fat sour cream

1 teaspoon salt

Pinch of freshly ground black pepper

SAUCE

¼ cup cornstarch

¼ cup water

2 tablespoons olive oil

1 medium yellow onion, finely chopped

1 pound mushrooms (such as cremini or button), woody stems trimmed and caps sliced

2 tablespoons dried Italian seasoning

1 teaspoon kosher salt

Pinch of freshly ground black pepper

¼ cup Worcestershire sauce or soy sauce

4 cups low-sodium beef broth

¼ cup grated Parmigiano-Reggiano cheese for topping

¼ cup finely chopped fresh flat-leaf parsley for garnish (optional)

1. *Make the noodles:* Preheat the oven to 350°F. Bring a large pot of generously salted water to boil over high heat. Add the noodles and cook for 3 minutes. Drain into a colander and rinse under cold running water to stop the cooking process.

2. Transfer the noodles to a large bowl. Add the brisket, sour cream, salt, and pepper and stir until the noodles are thoroughly coated. Transfer the noodles to a 9 by 13-inch lasagna or baking dish and set aside.

3. *Make the sauce:* In a small bowl, whisk together the cornstarch and water until the cornstarch dissolves and the mixture is a smooth slurry. Set aside.

4. In a large skillet, heat the oil over medium-high heat until shimmering. Add the onion and mushrooms and cook, stirring often, until the mushrooms release their liquid, the liquid evaporates, and the mushrooms are golden, about 6 minutes. Season with the Italian seasoning, salt, and pepper. Stir in the soy sauce and broth, then give the slurry a quick stir to recombine and stir it in as well. Raise the heat to high and bring the mixture to a boil. Turn down the heat to a simmer and cook, stirring often, until the sauce thickens, about 7 minutes.

5. *Bake the stroganoff:* Carefully pour the cooked sauce over the noodle mixture and, using a silicone spatula, fold in the sauce until well

Continued

Brisket Stroganoff, continued

mixed. Scatter the cheese evenly across the top. Bake, uncovered, until the top is browned and bubbly, about 20 minutes.

6. *To serve:* Remove from the oven and let cool for 10 minutes to allow the sauce to settle. Spoon onto individual plates and garnish with bright, fresh parsley—well, maybe garnish just your dish if green things are currently deemed "icky."

Notes: Assemble the stroganoff up to 1 day ahead and store covered in the fridge until ready to bake.

Prep the brisket in advance; see directions on page 109.

PREP-AHEAD ELEMENT(S)

SERVES 4

Rainbow Fried Rice

2 tablespoons olive oil

3 green onions, light green and white parts, finely chopped

2 garlic cloves, minced

½ red bell pepper, seeded and diced

½ orange bell pepper, seeded and diced

½ cup frozen shelled edamame

3 cups cooked jasmine rice, cold

1 cup diced fresh pineapple

1 tablespoon soy sauce

2 eggs, lightly beaten (optional)

Pinch of kosher salt, if adding eggs

Sweet pineapple, colorful peppers, and edamame make this a cheery lunch or dinner, with the edamame also adding welcome protein. You can also scramble in a couple of eggs for even more protein. Shortlist this dish as a prep-ahead go-to. Prepping the rice 1 day in advance will give the finished dish the chewy, crispy rice texture we all crave. Stash an extra batch of cooked, cooled rice in the freezer in an airtight container. Add the frozen rice to the skillet, increasing the cooking time by several minutes.

1. In a large nonstick skillet, warm 1 tablespoon of the oil over medium-high heat until shimmering. Add the green onions, garlic, red pepper, and orange pepper and cook, stirring often, until the peppers soften, about 3 minutes. Add the edamame and cook, stirring often, until the edamame thaw, about 1 minute. Transfer the pepper-edamame mixture to a medium bowl and set aside.

2. In the now-empty skillet, heat the remaining 1 tablespoon oil over medium-high heat until shimmering. Add the rice and spread in an even layer. Cook undisturbed until the bottom crisps slightly, about 1 minute.

3. Stir the pepper-edamame mixture and pineapple into the rice. Add the soy sauce and cook, stirring vigorously, until the rice is steaming hot, about 1 minute. Serve now or add eggs.

4. Push the rice to the sides of the skillet, making a well in the center. Add the eggs to the well, season with the salt, and scramble continuously until mostly set, about 1 minute. Incorporate the eggs into the rice and continue stirring everything together until the eggs are fully cooked, about 1 minute more. Serve now!

Note: Make the rice up to 1 day ahead. To prevent clumping, spread hot cooked rice on a sheet pan lined with a silicone baking sheet to cool. Store in an airtight container in the fridge.

Continued

Rainbow Fried Rice, continued

Rainbow Rice Rings Variation

Turn rainbow rice into 6 rice rings with a special Tupperware product. Here's how to wow: Preheat the oven to 375°F. In a medium bowl, stir together **1½ cups egg-free rainbow rice; 1 egg, lightly beaten;** and a **pinch of kosher salt.** Place a 6-cavity **SILICONE RING FORM** on a metal sheet pan. Divide the mixture evenly among the cups, using your fingers to pack in the mixture. Bake until the tops are lightly browned, about 12 minutes. Let rest for 5 minutes before popping out and serving.

PREP-AHEAD ELEMENT(S)

SERVES 4 TO 6

Chicken Kofta Slab Kebabs

2 pounds ground chicken

1 small red onion, minced

Leaves and tender stems from 1 small bunch flat-leaf parsley, minced

1½ teaspoons kosher salt

1 tablespoon garlic powder

1 teaspoon ground turmeric

1 teaspoon smoked paprika

3 tablespoons tomato paste

Olive oil for drizzling

SERVING SUGGESTIONS

Warm mini pita breads

Tzatziki, homemade (page 65) or store-bought

Pickles, homemade (page 79) or store-bought

Halved cherry tomatoes

Thinly sliced bell peppers (any color)

Hummus

Layered Greek Salad (page 65)

Plain cooked rice or pasta

Turkish kofta kebabs are traditionally made by forming seasoned minced meat into balls and then shaping each ball into an oval around a skewer for grilling. Skip the sharp skewers and make these slab kebabs. Serve them with warm mini pita, tzatziki or other dips, and (gasp!) SALAD! And if your little peeps are going through their "everything needs to be plain" phase of picky eating, terrifically delicious (but frankly nondescript-looking) kebabs with a side of plain rice or pasta will be a hit. And you can swap chicken for ground beef, lamb, or pork.

1. Preheat the oven to 400°F.

2. *Mix and shape the chicken mixture:* In a large bowl, combine the chicken, onion, parsley, salt, garlic powder, turmeric, paprika, and tomato paste. Using clean hands, mix until all the ingredients are evenly distributed.

3. Drizzle a 9 by 13-inch baking dish with olive oil. Transfer the chicken mixture to the dish. Using clean hands, press the mixture into an even layer. Using the edge of a silicone spatula, make nine equally spaced, shallow lengthwise cuts in the meat, taking care not to cut all the way through to the dish. Then make a shallow cut crosswise at the midpoint for a total of eighteen kebabs. You can further divide the kebabs into kofta bites, if you like.

4. Bake until the top is golden and the meat pulls away from the sides of the dish, about 12 minutes. Lower the oven temperature to 350°F and continue cooking until the juices run clear, about 5 minutes more.

5. *To serve:* Using the edge of the silicone spatula, cut into individual kebabs, using the pre-marked lines. Serve the kebabs in the baking dish with your choice of serving suggestions.

Notes: If making the tzatziki, you can do it up to 1 day ahead. The kids will enjoy helping you shred the cucumber with a grater.

Prep veggie sides, such as bell peppers, tomatoes, and cucumbers, up to 1 day ahead.

Eco Lunch Ideas

Bento-style containers are a win for families, the planet, and your lunch game. Kids love the divided compartments, and we love planet-friendly containers that will inspire you to break up with disposable bags for good.

The small and large **ECO+ LUNCH-IT** containers are perfect for packing wraps, pasta, salad, or rice in the large compartment and veggies, dip, bread, crackers, or a sweet treat in the smaller sections.

Need a bit of inspiration? Here's a taste of what could be for lunch.

IDEA #1

Large compartment:
Rainbow Fried Rice (page 173)

Two smaller compartments:
Halved grapes and nori sheets

IDEA #2

Large compartment:
Butter Bean Spread wrap (page 182)

Two smaller compartments:
Coconut macaroon (see page 194) and halved strawberries

IDEA #3

Large compartment:
Antipasto Affair (page 57)

Two smaller compartments:
Mango slices and buttered bread

IDEA #4

Large compartment:
Falafel Patties (page 145)

Two smaller compartments:
Cucumber slices and Baba Ghanoush (page 147) or hummus

IDEA #5

Large compartment:
Walnut, Cheddar, and Cherry Pepper Spread sandwich (page 182)

Two smaller compartments:
Orange wedges and pretzels

PREP UP TO
1 DAY AHEAD

SERVES 1 OR 2

Quick Wraps

One 10-inch tortilla wrap (such as spinach, whole wheat, or sun-dried tomato)

6 tablespoons spread (such as Butter Bean, Ham and Pickle, or Walnut, Cheddar, and Cherry Pepper, page 182), plus a bit more for sealing the wrap

SUGGESTED FILLINGS

¼ cup shredded cooked chicken (see page 112)

½ medium carrot, peeled and shredded

1 hard-boiled egg, finely chopped

2 lettuce leaves (such as romaine or butter)

6 cherry tomatoes, halved

¼ bell pepper (any color), halved, seeded, and cut into narrow strips

¼ cucumber, halved lengthwise, seeded, and cut into batons

¼ cup quick pickled vegetable(s) of choice (see page 79)

½ small avocado, peeled and sliced

Create flavor-packed wraps by using one of the fun savory spreads on page 182. Add favorite toppings, wrap, and serve. Or prep ahead for your child's school lunch by packing a whole wrap in a lunch box container.

1. Place the wrap on a clean work surface. Evenly cover the surface with your choice of spread, leaving a 1-inch border at the top edge.

2. Place or scatter up to four fillings over the top in an even layer, taking care not to overstuff.

3. Starting from the edge closest to you, roll up the wrap to enclose the fillings, stopping about 1 inch from the top. Apply a bit more spread to seal the seam. Fold in the open ends on the sides. Cut in half on the diagonal and enjoy now!

Note: Assemble the wraps up to 1 day ahead, but don't cut them to maintain freshness and texture. Store covered in the fridge and cut before serving.

PREP UP TO 3 DAYS AHEAD

EACH RECIPE MAKES ABOUT 1 CUP

Afternoon Spreads

These spreads are perfect for wraps, sandwiches, or as a tasty topping for crackers.

BUTTER BEAN SPREAD

- One 15½-ounce can butter beans, drained
- 3 tablespoons extra-virgin olive oil
- 1 teaspoon fresh lemon juice
- ¼ teaspoon garlic powder
- ¼ teaspoon kosher salt

In a food processor, combine the beans, oil, lemon juice, garlic powder, and salt and process until well mixed and smooth but with some texture.

Note: Store each spread in an airtight container in the fridge.

HAM AND PICKLE SPREAD

- 4 ounces sliced deli ham, torn into pieces
- 1 small dill pickle, coarsely chopped, plus 1 tablespoon brine
- 6 ounces cream cheese, at room temperature

In a food processor, combine the ham, pickle, and pickle brine and process until the ham and pickle are minced. Add the cream cheese, and process until well mixed.

WALNUT, CHEDDAR, AND CHERRY PEPPER SPREAD

- 12 walnut halves
- 6 sweet cherry peppers
- 1 cup shredded Cheddar cheese
- 2 ounces cream cheese, at room temperature

In a food processor, combine the walnuts, peppers, and cheese and process until the walnuts are finely ground. Add the cream cheese, and process until well mixed.

PREP UP TO
2 DAYS AHEAD

FREEZER-FRIENDLY
UP TO 3 MONTHS

MAKES 6 PIZZAS

Mini Deep-Dish Pizzas

PIZZA DOUGH

1 cup all-purpose flour

1 teaspoon baking powder

½ teaspoon kosher salt

¾ cup plain full-fat or 2-percent Greek yogurt

CHEESE FILLING

1¼ cups finely shredded provolone cheese

½ cup full-fat ricotta or cottage cheese

2 tablespoons finely grated Parmigiano-Reggiano cheese

6 tablespoons store-bought pizza sauce

24 pepperoni slices

These mini pizzas are a family favorite for both snacking and lunch boxes. The yogurt-based dough doesn't need rising time, and you can both mix and knead in the bowl! Build these minis just like a Chicago-style deep-dish pie: the gooey cheese layer goes on the bottom, then the sauce, pepperoni, and more cheese to cover the top. They disappear fast, so prep a double batch—you can even freeze them!

1. Preheat the oven to 375°F. Set a 6-cup silicone muffin form on a metal sheet pan.

2. *Make the dough:* In a large bowl, whisk together the flour, baking powder, and salt. Add the yogurt and, using a silicone spatula, mix slowly—so the flour doesn't fly everywhere—until thoroughly combined. Using your fingers, squeeze the dough together to form a ball. Then knead the dough ball in the bowl until soft and pliable, about 5 minutes.

3. Transfer the dough to a clean work surface and, using your fingers, divide it into six golf-ball-size portions. Roll each portion between your palms into a smooth ball, then flatten each ball into a round about ½ inch thick.

4. *Shape and partially bake the crusts:* Place one dough round in the center of each muffin cup. Starting from the center of a cup, use your fingers to press the dough outward, shaping it into an even crust that covers the bottom and extends up the sides. Repeat with the remaining cups. Partially bake the crusts until the edges are lightly browned, about 12 minutes.

5. Remove from the oven and, using the back of a spoon, press down on each crust to form a deep pocket. Set aside.

6. *Make the filling:* In a medium bowl, stir together ¾ cup of the provolone, the ricotta, and the Parmigiano-Reggiano cheeses until the mixture is fully blended and smooth.

Continued

Mini Deep-Dish Pizzas, continued

7. *Assemble and bake the pizzas:* Scoop about 1 tablespoon of the cheese mixture into each cup, pressing it down with the back of the spoon to compact it. Top each cup with 1 tablespoon of the pizza sauce, using the back of a spoon to smooth it to the edges. Top the sauce in each cup with four pepperoni slices. Scatter the remaining ½ cup provolone evenly over the tops.

8. Bake until the pepperoni slices are crispy and the cheese is browned, 18 to 20 minutes. Let cool for 15 minutes before unmolding and eating.

Note: Store the pizzas in an airtight container in the fridge. To reheat, place on a sheet pan and bake in the oven at 375°F until the cheese is melted and bubbly, 8 to 10 minutes. Or store in the freezer. Let the pizzas cool completely, then unmold and store them in a freezer-safe airtight container. To reheat from frozen, place on a sheet pan and bake in the oven at 400°F until the cheese is melted and bubbly, about 15 minutes.

PREP UP TO
2 DAYS AHEAD

MAKES 6 POPCORN CUPS

S'mores Popcorn Cups

- 6 tablespoons unsalted butter
- 3 cups mini marshmallows
- 3 cups plain popped popcorn
- 7 sheets graham crackers, crushed into fine crumbs (about 1 cup)
- ½ cup dark chocolate chips
- Neutral oil for your hands, plus 1 teaspoon
- 2 tablespoons white chocolate chips

These compact popcorn cups are bound with the classic s'mores concoction of melted marshmallow, chocolate, and graham cracker crumbs for an easy-to-hold, yummy-to-eat movie-night snack.

1. Have ready a 6-cup silicone muffin form. In a medium saucepan, melt the butter over medium heat. Stir in the marshmallows and heat, stirring often, until they are mostly melted, about 1 minute. Remove from the heat and continue stirring until completely melted.

2. Add the popcorn and graham cracker crumbs and stir until the popcorn is thoroughly coated. Add the dark chocolate chips and stir until melted.

3. Grease your hands with a bit of oil to prevent sticking. Then use your hands to divide the mixture evenly among the muffin cups, pressing and packing it down. Set aside.

4. In a small microwave-safe bowl, combine the white chocolate chips and the 1 teaspoon oil. Microwave on 50 percent power in 20-second bursts, stirring after each burst, until the chocolate is melted and smooth.

5. Drizzle the melted chocolate over the popcorn cups. Refrigerate for 10 minutes to set. Pop the cups out of the mold and enjoy!

Note: Store the cups in an airtight container at room temperature.

PREP UP TO
2 DAYS AHEAD

SERVES 1 TO 2

Fudgy Brownie Baby Cake

- 2 ounces bittersweet baking chocolate (60% cacao), coarsely chopped
- 3 tablespoons unsalted butter, cubed
- ¼ cup packed light brown sugar
- ¼ teaspoon pure vanilla extract
- 1 egg yolk, at room temperature
- ¼ cup all-purpose flour
- 2 tablespoons unsweetened cocoa powder
- ⅛ teaspoon baking powder
- Pinch of kosher salt
- 2 tablespoons milk chocolate chips
- Vanilla ice cream for serving
- Maraschino cherries for serving (optional)

Make this little cake as a sweet treat to share with your kiddo—or keep it all to yourself after a long week (we won't tell). Baked in a silicone round cake form, it turns out irresistibly rich and moist. Top the cake with ice cream and cherries for brownie cake à la mode. Triple the recipe and batch bake three cakes at once, placing the cake forms on a large metal sheet pan for baking. To make a brownie layer cake, spread the top of each cake with chocolate frosting and stack!

1. Preheat the oven to 350°F. Place a 6-inch silicone round cake form on a metal sheet pan.

2. Fill a small saucepan two-thirds full with water and bring to a gentle simmer over medium-low heat. Put the chocolate, butter, brown sugar, and vanilla into a large heatproof bowl and set it on top of the saucepan, making sure the bottom of the bowl does not touch the water. Stir continuously until the mixture is smooth, 1 to 2 minutes. Remove from the heat and set aside to cool for 10 minutes.

3. Add the egg yolk to the chocolate mixture and whisk until well mixed. Sift the flour, cocoa powder, baking powder, and salt into the chocolate mixture and, using a silicone spatula, fold in just until no streaks of flour or cocoa powder remain. Fold in the chocolate chips.

4. Transfer the batter to the cake form, spreading it evenly. Bake until a toothpick inserted into the center comes out clean, 12 to 14 minutes.

5. Transfer to a wire cooling rack and let cool in the mold for 10 minutes before unmolding onto a serving plate. Top with vanilla ice cream and cherries (if using) and enjoy now!

Notes: Save the egg white for making Chocolate-Dipped Coconut Macaroons (page 194).

Store the cake in an airtight container in the fridge. Reheat in the microwave at 50 percent power for 30 seconds to serve warm, if desired.

PREP UP TO
1 WEEK AHEAD

FREEZER-FRIENDLY
UP TO 3 MONTHS

SERVES 6 TO 8

Raspberry Frozen Yogurt Bark

Thanks to yogurt and fresh raspberries, this bark is a refreshing, sweet, and tart cold snack or after-dinner treat. Kids can even create their own "signature" toppings! To keep the peace, decorate the raspberry yogurt base in quadrants, making four flavors in one. Break into pieces so everyone gets their favorite.

RASPBERRY YOGURT BASE

1 cup fresh raspberries (6 ounces)

1 teaspoon fresh lemon juice

2 cups plain full-fat Greek yogurt

2 tablespoons maple syrup

SUGGESTED TOPPINGS

Mini white or semisweet chocolate chips

Finely chopped fresh fruit (such as strawberries or pineapple) or whole blueberries

Mini marshmallows

Unsweetened finely shredded desiccated coconut

Finely chopped nuts (such as almonds or pecans)

1. Line a metal sheet pan with a silicone baking sheet.

2. *Make the base:* In a medium bowl, combine the raspberries and lemon juice. Using a masher, crush the raspberries until reduced to a puree. Add the yogurt and maple syrup and stir until well mixed.

3. Using a silicone spatula, spread the yogurt mixture in an even, thin layer (about ¼ inch) on the baking sheet. Top as you wish from the list of toppings.

4. Place the sheet pan in the freezer until the bark is solid, about 4 hours. Remove from the freezer, break the bark into pieces, and enjoy!

Note: Store the broken bark pieces in the freezer.

PREP UP TO
3 DAYS AHEAD

MAKES 32 COOKIES

Chocolate-Dipped Coconut Macaroons

2½ cups unsweetened finely shredded desiccated coconut

One 14-ounce can sweetened condensed milk

1 teaspoon vanilla extract

Pinch of kosher salt

2 egg whites (see Notes)

⅔ cup finely chopped bittersweet baking chocolate (60%)

1 tablespoon coconut oil

This decadent recipe involves the whole family: get the older kids or adults to whip the egg whites, while the little ones can scoop the cookie dough (or at least "plop" the rolled dough onto the sheet pan) and make a satisfying mess covering the cookies with melted chocolate. These macaroons will go quickly, so you might as well make a double (or triple!) batch.

1. *Make the dough:* In a medium bowl, stir together the coconut, condensed milk, vanilla, and salt.

2. In a small bowl, using a handheld mixer, beat the egg whites on medium speed until foamy. Increase the speed to medium-high and beat until stiff peaks form.

3. Using a silicone spatula, fold the egg whites into the coconut mixture until well incorporated. Cover and refrigerate for 30 minutes. This helps firm the dough for scooping and dropping.

4. While the dough chills, preheat the oven to 325°F. Line a metal sheet pan with a silicone baking sheet.

5. *Bake and dip the cookies:* Using a 1-tablespoon cookie scoop, drop dough balls onto the silicone baking sheet, spacing them about 2 inches apart. Bake until the bottoms are golden and the tops are lightly browned, 12 to 15 minutes. Let cool completely on the baking sheet on a wire cooling rack, then use a silicone spatula to lift them off the baking sheet and onto a clean work surface.

6. In a small microwave-safe bowl, combine the chocolate and oil. Microwave on 50 percent power in 20-second bursts, stirring after each burst, until the chocolate is melted and smooth. Dip half of each cooled macaroon in the chocolate, letting the excess drip off, then place the macaroon back on the baking sheet. When all the macaroons have been dipped, drizzle any remaining chocolate over the tops. Refrigerate for 15 minutes to set the chocolate.

7. Peel the macaroons off the baking sheet and enjoy now.

Notes: Save the egg yolks to add to Coffee Shop–Style Cheddar Bacon Egg Bites (page 39) or Fine Herb and Feta Omelet (page 46).

Store the macaroons in an airtight container at room temperature.

Tupperware®

Tupperware
Tupperware

Party People!

"Whenever I cook, I save all my scraps—onion skins, potato and carrot peels, asparagus ends, even the bones from a roasted chicken. Instead of tossing them, I collect everything in my Extra Large Silicone Bag and freeze as I go. Once the bag is full, I use my Pressure Cooker to turn it into the most delicious, nutrient-rich homemade stock—zero waste, all flavor!"

—PAULINE B.,
9 YEARS SELLING TUPPERWARE PRODUCTS

The secret to a great party is bringing people together with a spread that is not only delicious but also looks stunning—without the cook breaking a sweat. These easy recipes do the heavy lifting so you can relax and enjoy the fun. Your friends will be convinced that you have a catering team behind the scenes.

Inspired by the charm of retro Tupperware recipes, this chapter offers fresh ideas, from Pink Pickled Eggs (page 206) and plant-based Grape Jelly "Meat" Balls (page 223) to prep-ahead dinner-party mains like Lemon Ricotta Shells with Melted Cherry Tomatoes (page 203) and Herb Roasted Chicken (page 200), plus sweets and treats for all occasions.

- Need a bunch of citrus juice for recipes like Lemon Ricotta Shells with Melted Cherry Tomatoes (page 203)? Reach for the multipurpose **ZEST 'N PRESS** gadget to remove every bit of zest and extract every drop of juice into your recipe.

- The **LARGE SPATULA** is angled and extra wide for steady flip jobs, like flipping over the delicious Strawberry Crunch Ice Cream Bars (page 231).

- Use the **SUPERSONIC CHOPPER COMPACT** to mince the shallot in Grape Jelly "Meat" Balls (page 223) or anytime you need finely chopped herbs, nuts, and other mix-ins.

SERVES 6

Herb Roasted Chicken

2 lemons, zest grated, then thinly sliced

2 large yellow onions, thinly sliced

One 3½-pound chicken, patted dry

¼ cup olive oil, or as needed

Kosher salt and freshly ground black pepper

¼ cup mixed finely chopped fresh rosemary, sage, and thyme, in equal amounts, plus 3 thyme sprigs

2 garlic cloves

Kale au gratin (see page 89) for serving (optional)

Pull together a whole, juicy roasted chicken for an impromptu dinner party in a snap. The sliced lemon and onion beneath the chicken release their natural juices, basting the bird and infusing it with bright flavor.

1. Preheat the oven to 425°F.

2. Scatter the lemon and onion slices in the bottom of a 9 by 13-inch baking dish and place the chicken, breast-side up, on top.

3. Generously rub the chicken all over with the oil, then season generously with the salt, pepper, lemon zest, and chopped herbs, coating evenly. Stuff the cavity with the thyme sprigs and garlic cloves.

4. Transfer the chicken to the oven and cook, uncovered, until the skin is golden brown and an instant-read thermometer inserted into the thickest part of a thigh away from bone registers 165°F or the juices run clear when the thigh is pierced, about 1 hour. Remove from the oven and let rest for 10 minutes before carving.

5. *To serve:* Transfer the chicken to a serving platter and spoon the pan juices over the top. Serve with the kale au gratin, if desired.

PREP UP TO
1 DAY AHEAD

FREEZER-FRIENDLY
UP TO 3 MONTHS

SERVES 6 TO 8

Lemon Ricotta Shells with Melted Cherry Tomatoes

The light, fragrant sauce of these stuffed shells celebrates summer tomatoes, while the tangy lemon ricotta filling shines on its own or pairs perfectly with summer veggies. Heads will turn after one mouthwatering bite, and someone's bound to ask, "Who made these?" Raise your hand—they're on to you, meal prep star.

SAUCE

¼ cup extra-virgin olive oil

6 garlic cloves, minced

3 pints tricolor cherry tomatoes (about 2 pounds), halved (leave tiny tomatoes whole)

4 fresh basil leaves

1 teaspoon kosher salt

1 cup water

SHELLS

One 1-pound package jumbo shells (about 40 shells)

Olive oil for drizzling

One 32-ounce container whole-milk ricotta cheese

½ cup finely grated Parmigiano-Reggiano cheese, plus more for garnish

2 tablespoons fresh thyme leaves

Grated zest of 1 lemon

1 teaspoon kosher salt

1. Preheat the oven to 375°F.

2. *Make the sauce:* In a large skillet, heat the oil over medium-high heat. Add the garlic and cook, stirring often, until fragrant, about 1 minute. Add the tomatoes, basil, salt, and water and bring the mixture to a boil. Turn down the heat to low and cook, stirring now and then, until the tomatoes soften and some of the liquid in the pan has reduced, 15 to 18 minutes. Remove from the heat and set aside.

3. *Prep the shells:* Bring a large pot of generously salted water to a boil over high heat. Add the shells and cook until they start to open, about 4 minutes. Drain into a colander and rinse under cold running water to stop the cooking process. Drizzle the shells with oil and toss to prevent sticking. Set aside to cool.

4. *Prep the filling:* In a large bowl, combine the ricotta, Parmigiano-Reggiano, thyme, lemon zest, and salt and stir to mix well.

5. *Stuff the shells:* Pour about ¾ cup of the tomato sauce onto the bottom of a 9 by 13-inch baking dish. Fill each shell with about 1 tablespoon of the ricotta mixture. As you work, arrange twenty-eight of the shells in a single layer in the prepared pan. Pour 1½ cups of the tomato sauce over the top. Stuff the remaining twelve shells and layer them on top. You may have some filling left over; set it aside for spooning over the top in the last 10 minutes of baking. Pour the remaining sauce over the top.

Continued

Lemon Ricotta Shells with Melted Cherry Tomatoes, continued

6. *To bake and serve:* Cover the dish and bake for 30 minutes. Remove from the oven and remove the cover. Increase the oven temperature to 400°F. Sprinkle the top evenly with Parmigiano-Reggiano and spoon any remaining ricotta over the top. Return the pan, uncovered, to the oven. Bake until the ricotta cheese is bubbly, about 10 minutes more. Let sit for 15 minutes before serving.

Note: Assemble the shells, then freeze for later before baking. Bake, covered, from frozen in the oven at 350°F until warmed through, 30 to 35 minutes.

Veggie Stuffed Shells Variation

To create veggie-stuffed shells, combine **1 cup lightly steamed sweet corn kernels or chopped broccoli, mushrooms, zucchini, or spinach** with the **ricotta mixture.**

PREP UP TO
1 DAY AHEAD

MAKES 12 DEVILED EGGS

Pink Pickled Eggs

6 eggs

One 15-ounce can sliced beets (see Notes)

1 cup apple cider vinegar

2 green onions, light green and white parts, finely chopped

¼ cup mayonnaise

2 teaspoons tahini

1 teaspoon Dijon mustard

Pinch of ground turmeric

Pinch of kosher salt

Sesame seeds for garnish

Finely chopped fresh herb (such as flat-leaf parsley, oregano, or dill) for garnish (optional)

These beet juice–pickled deviled eggs boast a vibrant, sassy pink color and a tangy kick that cuts through the silky-rich deviled-egg filling, made even creamier with a spoonful of tahini. A sprinkle of sesame seeds adds a delightful crunch, complementing the tahini's nutty flavor—such pretty little devils. Pickle the eggs up to 1 day in advance to turn them a very bright pink.

1. Gently place the eggs in a medium saucepan and add water to cover by 1 inch. Set the pot over high heat and bring to a boil. Turn down the heat to medium and set the timer for 8 minutes. Meanwhile, fill a large bowl with ice water.

2. When the eggs are ready, using a slotted spoon, transfer the eggs to the ice bath to stop the cooking process. Let the eggs sit for 5 minutes. Meanwhile, open the can of beets and drain into a fine-mesh strainer placed over a small bowl. Save the beets for another use (see Notes). Add the vinegar to the beet juice and stir to mix.

3. One at a time, peel the eggs under cold running water and transfer them to a medium bowl. Pour the beet juice mixture over the eggs. Cover and refrigerate for at least 6 hours or up to overnight. Their color will range from light to bright pink, depending on how long they are soaked.

4. Remove the eggs from the beet mixture and pat dry. Cut each egg in half lengthwise. Gently scoop the yolk out of each half and drop into a medium bowl. Set the egg whites, hollow-side up, on a large plate or platter.

5. To the bowl with the yolks, add half of the green onions, the mayonnaise, tahini, mustard, turmeric, and salt. Mash with the broad paddle of a silicone spatula until smooth and creamy. Taste and adjust the seasoning with salt if needed.

6. Spoon the filling into each egg half, mounding the top. Sprinkle with sesame seeds and garnish with the remaining green onions and herb (if using), then serve.

Notes: Store the unused beets in an airtight container in the fridge. Julienne the reserved beets for Beet, Bulgur, and Blue Cheese (page 70).

Store the pickled eggs in an airtight container in the fridge.

PREP UP TO
2 DAYS AHEAD

MAKES 16 TOPPED BLINI

Blini with Caramelized Shallot Cream Cheese

- ¾ cup all-purpose flour
- 1 teaspoon baking powder
- ¼ teaspoon kosher salt
- ¼ cup full-fat cottage cheese
- 2 tablespoons unsalted butter, melted, plus 1 to 2 tablespoons for cooking
- ⅓ cup whole or 2-percent milk
- 1 egg
- Shallot Cream Cheese (recipe follows)

SERVING SUGGESTIONS

- Pastrami or roast beef slices, chopped dill pickle, or Any Quick Pickle (page 79) of choice
- Fresh or dried fig, mixed fresh herbs, olive oil drizzle
- ½ jammy egg (see page 81), smoked paprika, capers
- Smoked salmon, thinly sliced cucumber, fresh dill
- Smoked trout, julienned beets

These tender two-bite pancakes are inspired by traditional Eastern European buckwheat flour blini but come together more quickly because they don't call for a yeasted batter. Spread them with whipped shallot cream cheese (or plop on dollops of sour cream or crème fraîche), then add savory or sweet colorful toppings, from smoked salmon and cucumbers and fresh figs and herbs to pastrami. Double or triple the batter as needed to make more blini.

1. *Make the blini:* In a medium bowl, whisk together the flour, baking powder, and salt. In a blender, combine the cottage cheese, melted butter, milk, and egg and blend on high speed until smooth, about 20 seconds. Add to the flour mixture and whisk until a smooth, thick batter forms.

2. Have ready a wire cooling rack. In the reserved skillet, melt 1 tablespoon butter over medium heat, then tilt the pan to coat the bottom evenly. For each blini, spoon 1 tablespoon of the batter into the pan, adding as many will fit while leaving room for flipping. Cook undisturbed until bubbles form on the surface, 2 to 3 minutes. Flip and cook until the undersides are golden, 1 to 2 minutes more. Transfer the blini to the wire rack. Repeat with the remaining batter in one or two batches, melting additional butter if needed to prevent sticking.

3. *To serve:* Spread a bit of shallot cream over the top of each blini and top as you wish. Serve now.

Note: Store the blini in an airtight container in the fridge. To reheat, warm them in a skillet over low heat until just heated through.

Continued

Blini with Caramelized Shallot Cream Cheese, continued

Shallot Cream Cheese

PREP UP TO 2 DAYS AHEAD
MAKES ABOUT 1 CUP

1 tablespoon olive oil
1 teaspoon unsalted butter
5 medium shallots, thinly sliced
½ teaspoon kosher salt
One 8-ounce package cream cheese, at room temperature
½ teaspoon garlic powder
¼ teaspoon freshly ground black pepper
¼ cup whole milk

This shallot cream cheese is also the base for French Onion Dip (page 214)—how great!

1. In a medium nonstick skillet, heat the oil and butter over medium heat until the butter melts. Add the shallots and salt and turn down the heat to low. Cook, stirring often, until the shallots are soft and browned, about 20 minutes. Transfer to a medium bowl, then wipe out the skillet and set aside.

2. To the bowl with the shallots, add the cream cheese, garlic powder, pepper, and milk. Using a handheld mixer, beat on low speed until smooth. Set aside.

Note: Store the cream cheese in an airtight container in the fridge. Let it sit out to bring to room temperature, about 30 minutes. Stir before using.

Deep Dip Dive

Need an instant hit for your next gathering? Try one or dive into creating all of these make-ahead dip recipes for your next shindig.

Chocolate Miso Fondue

PREP UP TO 2 DAYS AHEAD
SERVES 4 TO 6

FONDUE

1½ cups heavy cream

1 cup dark or semisweet chocolate chips

2 teaspoons white miso paste

FOR SERVING

Assorted fresh fruits (such as strawberries, orange wedges, grapes, and apple slices)

Pretzels or pretzel rods (thin or thick)

Assorted cookies (such as shortbread, wafers, or biscotti)

Graham crackers

Marshmallows

An unexpected addition of white miso paste gives this easy chocolate ganache buttery depth and a slightly salty flavor. This recipe lends itself to an elevated and interactive dessert station: set out a bunch of beautiful containers with an assortment of fresh fruits, pretzels, marshmallows, and cookies and let your guests get to dipping!

1. *Make the fondue:* Place the chocolate chips in a heatproof medium bowl.

2. In a small saucepan, warm the cream over low heat until it just begins to simmer. As soon as you see gentle bubbles form around the edge of the pan, remove the pan from the heat and pour the cream over the chocolate chips.

3. Let the mixture stand until the chips are melted, about 5 minutes. Add the miso and gently whisk until the mixture is smooth and creamy. Use a silicone spatula to transfer the mixture to a shallow serving bowl.

4. *To serve:* Set the bowl in the center of a large serving platter surrounded by your favorite fresh fruits and other treats. Dip pretzels, cookies, and graham crackers by hand and use fondue skewers or forks for dipping fruits and marshmallows.

Note: Store the fondue in an airtight container in the fridge. To reheat, microwave at 50 percent power in 20-second bursts, stirring after each burst, until loose and warmed through.

PREP UP TO 2 DAYS AHEAD

SERVES 12

3½ cups shredded Cheddar cheese (from two 8-ounce blocks)

¼ cup chopped fresh cilantro

One 2¼-ounce can sliced black olives, drained

¼ cup drained canned fire-roasted diced green chiles

1½ cups homemade or store-bought guacamole

One 8-ounce package cream cheese, at room temperature, cubed

1 cup full-fat sour cream

2 teaspoons taco seasoning

One 15-ounce can sweet corn kernels, drained

2 cups Vegetarian Refried Beans (page 108), or one 16-ounce can vegetarian refried beans

3 tablespoons whole or 2-percent milk

1 cup crushed tortilla chips, plus sturdy whole chips for serving

Fiesta Dip

Layer freshly shredded cheese, olives, fire-roasted peppers, zesty guacamole, spiced sour cream, sweet corn, and creamy refried beans to create this decadent Mexican-inspired party dip. This recipe uses the **JEL PARTY** mold to show off the colorful layers.

1. Insert the core seal in the middle of the **JEL PARTY** mold and lightly grease the form with neutral oil, making sure to get in all the crevices. (Omit this step if making the dip in a 9 by 13-inch glass baking dish.)

2. In a small bowl, combine 3 cups of the Cheddar cheese, the cilantro, and olives and mix well. Spread the mixture in the mold, pressing it firmly into the sides.

3. Scatter the green chiles over the cheese layer. Spread the guacamole over the chiles in an even layer.

4. In a medium bowl, using a handheld mixer, beat together the cream cheese, sour cream, and taco seasoning on low speed until smooth. Using a silicone spatula, fold in the corn, distributing it evenly. Spread the mixture over the guacamole in an even layer.

5. In a medium nonstick skillet, combine the refried beans and milk over low heat, stirring, until the mixture is loose and creamy, about 30 seconds. Add the remaining ½ cup Cheddar cheese and stir until the cheese melts, a few seconds more. Remove from the heat and allow to cool for a few minutes, then spread evenly over the cream cheese layer. Scatter the crushed chips over the bean layer. Cover and refrigerate for at least 4 hours or up to overnight.

6. When ready to serve, flip the mold so the cover is on the bottom. You will use the cover as the serving dish. Slowly remove the middle insert. The dip will release naturally. Serve with tortilla chips and a serving spoon so guests can either scoop or transfer a portion onto their plate.

Note: You can make this dip in a 9 by 13-inch clear glass baking dish. Just layer the ingredients in reverse order, starting with the tortilla chips on the bottom, followed by the refried beans with cheese, then the cream cheese mixture, guacamole, and green chiles, and then finish with shredded cheese, cilantro, and olives.

Store the fiesta dip covered in the fridge. Serve cold.

French Onion Dip

PREP UP TO 2 DAYS AHEAD
SERVES 6

1 recipe Shallot Cream Cheese (see page 210), at room temperature

½ cup full-fat sour cream

1 teaspoon smoked paprika

Kosher salt

Potato chips for serving

Classic French onion dip gets a makeover with the sweet, mellow onion flavor of caramelized shallots. Serve in a **CHIP 'N DIP** set for extra vintage flair.

In a medium bowl, combine the shallot cream cheese, sour cream, and paprika and stir until smooth. Season to taste with salt. Serve with potato chips for dipping.

Note: Store the French onion dip in an airtight container in the fridge. Let it sit out for 20 minutes to soften then stir before using.

Buffalo Chicken Dip

PREP UP TO 1 DAY AHEAD
SERVES 6 TO 8

One 8-ounce package cream cheese, cubed, at room temperature

1 cup ranch dressing

1 cup Buffalo sauce, homemade (page 113) or store-bought

1 tablespoon garlic powder

2 tablespoons pickle brine

2 green onions, light green and white parts, finely chopped

4 cups shredded cooked chicken (see page 112)

2 cups shredded Cheddar cheese (from one 8-ounce block)

Celery sticks for serving

This gooey chicken dip, with a tangy twist from pickle brine, bakes beautifully, so feel free to serve it straight from the oven in style—use a shallow tray or bowl for celery sticks. Short on time? Purchase a rotisserie chicken, discard the skin and bones, and shred the meat into bite-size pieces.

1. Preheat the oven to 350°F.

2. In a medium saucepan, combine the cream cheese, ranch dressing, and Buffalo sauce over medium-low heat and cook, whisking continuously, until the cream cheese melts and the mixture is smooth and creamy, 5 to 7 minutes. Remove from the heat.

3. Stir in the garlic powder, brine, green onions, and chicken until the chicken is well coated. Stir in 1 cup of the cheese.

4. Transfer the mixture to a 2-quart or 9 by 9-inch baking dish. Scatter the remaining 1 cup cheese across the top. Bake until the top is golden and bubbling, 20 to 22 minutes. Remove from the oven and let rest for 10 minutes before serving with celery sticks for dipping.

Note: Assemble the dip 1 day ahead and store the covered baking dish in the fridge. When ready to bake, add 10 minutes to the cooking time.

Pitcher Sippers

PREP UP TO 1 DAY AHEAD
SERVES 10 TO 12

Rose Iced Tea

12 cups brewed and chilled hibiscus tea
½ cup rose water
½ cup honey
Food-grade dried rose petals, for garnish

Combine the tea, rose water, and honey in a 4-quart jar. Stir until the honey dissolves, then chill. Serve over ice and garnish with the rose petals.

Virgin Grapefruit Paloma

8 cups grapefruit juice
1 cup fresh lime juice
½ cup honey
Club soda
Fresh mint sprigs, for garnish

Combine the grapefruit juice, lime juice, and honey in a 3-quart pitcher. Stir until the honey dissolves, then chill. Serve over ice, top off with club soda, and garnish with mint sprigs.

Classic Margarita

1 (750-ml) bottle tequila
1 cup fresh lime juice
½ cup triple sec
½ cup honey
Lime wedges
Kosher salt, for garnish

Combine the tequila, lime juice, triple sec, and honey in a 3-quart pitcher. Stir until the honey dissolves, then chill. Wet glass rims with the lime wedges and dip in the salt. Serve over ice.

Fruity Sangria

1 (750-ml) bottle red or white wine
½ cup gin
1 cup fresh orange juice
2 tablespoons honey
1 cup diced pineapple
1 orange, thinly sliced
1 lemon, thinly sliced
4 cups ginger ale
Fresh strawberries, thinly sliced, for garnish

Combine the wine, gin, orange juice, honey, pineapple, orange, and lemon in a 3-quart pitcher. Stir until well mixed and the honey dissolves, then chill. Just before serving, stir in the ginger ale. Serve over ice and garnish with sliced strawberries.

PREP UP TO
1 DAY AHEAD

SERVES 6

Kimchi Mac 'n' Tuna Salad

1 cup spicy kimchi, finely chopped

1 medium red onion, minced

Two 5-ounce cans tuna packed in oil, drained and finely chopped

8 fresh basil leaves, torn into small pieces, plus 1 small bunch for garnish (optional)

2 cups cooked elbow macaroni, cooled

1 cup shredded cheese (such as sharp Cheddar, Gruyère, or fontina)

1 cup mayonnaise

Kosher salt

This retro-inspired macaroni and tuna salad gets a spicy flavor upgrade from kimchi, the salted, fermented staple of the Korean table. Finely chop each ingredient to ensure the flavors and textures meld. If you don't own a JEL-RING mold, serve the salad from a bowl and scoop it into lettuce cups. Mix and mold it (1 day) in advance. Chill it, serve it, and watch your guests fight over seconds.

1. Lightly grease a 5¼-cup ring mold with a lid with neutral oil, making sure to get in all the crevices.

2. In a medium bowl, combine the kimchi, onion, tuna, basil, macaroni, and cheese and stir to mix. Add the mayonnaise and stir until all the ingredients are evenly coated. Season to taste with salt.

3. Transfer the mixture to the prepared ring mold. Cover and refrigerate for at least 2 hours or up to 1 day.

4. *To serve:* Flip the mold so the lid is now on the bottom. This is how you'll serve the salad. The structure holds together, making it easy to scoop. Gently remove the middle insert. The salad will release naturally. Set a bunch of fresh basil leaves in the center of the mold, if desired, and serve now!

PREP AHEAD ELEMENT(S)

PREP UP TO
2 DAYS AHEAD

SERVES 4 TO 6

Spiced Yogurt Baked Salmon

2 tablespoons light brown sugar

1 teaspoon kosher salt

One 1½-pound skin-on salmon side

¾ cup plain full-fat Greek yogurt

1 tablespoon curry powder

½ teaspoon garlic powder

¼ teaspoon ground sumac (optional)

¼ teaspoon ground ginger

Finely chopped fresh herb (such as dill, oregano, or mint) for garnish

Peachy Green with Goat Cheese and Nut Clusters (page 58) or Roasted Cabbage, Apricot Lentils, and Harissa Yogurt (page 135) for serving

Slathering a side of salmon with curry-spiced yogurt keeps the fish moist and adds a terrific aroma and India-inspired flavor. A garnish of fresh herbs gives it a burst of color and brightness. Serve the salmon with a great side and you've got a beautiful meal for company.

1. Preheat the oven to 400°F. Line a metal sheet pan with a silicone baking sheet.

2. In a small bowl, stir together the sugar and salt. Lay the salmon, skin-side down, on the prepared sheet pan and rub the sugar mixture over the flesh to coat evenly. Let sit for 15 minutes. The rub will release moisture and firm the texture of the fish.

3. In a medium bowl, stir together the yogurt, curry powder, garlic powder, sumac (if using), and ginger.

4. Pat the salmon dry of any excess moisture. Slather the yogurt over the top to cover. Bake until the flesh flakes easily with a fork, 18 to 20 minutes. Transfer the salmon to a serving platter and garnish with the herbs.

5. *To serve:* Cut the fillet into four to six equal pieces and serve alongside your side of choice.

Notes: Store the salmon in an airtight container in the fridge. Serve cold, flaked salmon for a brunch spread.

Prep the spiced yogurt up to 2 days ahead and refrigerate in an airtight container.

PREP UP TO
1 DAY AHEAD

FREEZER-FRIENDLY
UP TO 3 MONTHS

MAKES ABOUT 60 MEATBALLS

Grape Jelly "Meat" Balls

"MEAT" BALLS

1 tablespoon flaxseed meal

2½ tablespoons water

2 pounds plant-based ground meat (not crumbles!)

1 large shallot, minced

2 teaspoons garlic powder

¼ teaspoon freshly ground black pepper

½ cup panko bread crumbs

2 tablespoons olive oil, plus more if needed

SAUCE

1½ cups grape jelly

1 cup chili sauce

1½ teaspoons kosher salt

¼ teaspoon freshly ground black pepper

These sweet and tangy cocktail meatballs are proof that classics can evolve. The recipe calls for plant-based meat and a flax "egg" (an easy-to-make egg substitute) to help bind the mixture. And because faux meatballs have a neutral flavor, you can use them as a meatless alternative in any menu that calls for meatballs—from pasta night to toasty sandwiches.

1. *Make the flax egg:* In a small bowl, whisk together the flaxseed meal and water. Let sit for 5 minutes to thicken.

2. *Make the meatballs:* Have ready a silicone baking sheet. In a medium bowl, combine the plant-based meat, shallot, garlic powder, pepper, panko, and flax egg and stir to mix well. To shape each cocktail-size meatball, scoop up 1½ teaspoons of the mixture, lightly wet your hands, roll the mixture into a compact ball, and set aside on the baking sheet.

3. Have ready a large plate. When all the balls are shaped, in a large nonstick skillet, heat the oil over medium-high heat until shimmering. Add as many balls to the pan in a single layer as will fit without crowding and cook, gently shaking the pan often to turn the balls, until browned on all sides and firm, 2 to 3 minutes. Transfer to the plate. Repeat with the remaining meatballs in one or two batches, adding more oil if needed to prevent sticking. Once all the meatballs are browned, return them to the skillet.

4. *Make the sauce:* Add the jelly, chili sauce, salt, and pepper to the skillet and continue cooking the meatballs, stirring now and then, until a smooth sauce forms and the meatballs are cooked through, 5 to 7 minutes more.

5. *To serve:* Transfer the meatballs to a serving platter and spoon the sauce over the top. Serve now with toothpicks alongside for easy grabbing.

Note: Store the meatballs in the sauce in an airtight container in the fridge. To reheat: Place the meatballs and sauce plus ¼ cup of water in a saucepan and warm over low heat. Cover and simmer, stirring occasionally, until heated through, about 15 minutes. Uncooked meatballs freeze beautifully! Arrange them in a single layer on a metal sheet pan lined with a silicone baking sheet and freeze for 2 hours, then transfer to a freezer-safe container and return to the freezer. Thaw the meatballs in the fridge overnight before cooking.

PREP UP TO
2 DAYS AHEAD

SERVES 6

No-Bake Lavender and Honey Cheesecake

CHEESECAKE

One ¼-ounce packet (2½ teaspoons) unflavored gelatin

1 cup heavy cream

Two 8-ounce packages cream cheese, at room temperature

½ cup honey

1 teaspoon lavender extract paste (see Notes, page 227)

2 or 3 drops purple gel food coloring (optional)

GRAHAM CRACKER CRUST

8 sheets graham crackers, finely crushed (about 1 cup)

6 tablespoons unsalted butter, melted

Pinch of salt

Edible flowers or herbs (such as lavender, pansies, violas, borage blossoms, mint, and arugula; see Notes, page 227) for garnish

It's true that "we eat first with our eyes." This romantic, vintage-inspired cheesecake made in the JEL-RING mold is a captivating treat that is meant to be admired—think birthdays and baby showers! The all-natural lavender paste infuses the cake with a delicate floral flavor with hints of mint and rosemary, balanced by the sweetness of honey. To make this cake even more special, adorn it with edible flowers before serving.

1. Insert the core seal in the middle of the JEL-RING mold and lightly grease the form with neutral oil, making sure to get in all the crevices.

2. *Make the cheesecake:* In a microwave-safe container, whisk together the gelatin and ¼ cup of the heavy cream until well combined. Set aside to bloom for 1 minute. Then microwave on 100 percent power for 15 seconds to liquefy. Set aside to cool.

3. In a small bowl, using a handheld mixer, whip the remaining ¾ cup cream on low speed and gradually increase to medium-high until stiff peaks form. Set aside. Rinse and dry the mixer beaters.

4. In a medium bowl, using the mixer, beat together the cream cheese and honey on low speed until well mixed. Add the lavender paste and reserved gelatin and beat on low speed until well incorporated. Add the whipped cream and food coloring (if using) and continue beating on low speed until the mixture is fluffy, the lavender color is uniform, and no white streaks remain.

5. Spread the mixture evenly in the prepared mold, then tap the mold on the counter a few times to settle the mixture. Seal and refrigerate until firm, 4 to 5 hours.

Continued

No-Bake Lavender and Honey Cheesecake, continued

6. *Once firm, prepare the graham cracker crust:* In a medium bowl, stir together the graham cracker crumbs, butter, and salt until the consistency of wet sand. Unseal the mold and use your fingers to gently press the crumb mixture evenly on top of the chilled cake. Reseal and refrigerate until the crust is firm, about 1½ hours.

7. *To serve:* Flip the mold so the lid is now on the bottom. Let sit for 10 minutes to soften slightly. Gently remove the middle insert. The cheesecake will release naturally. Slide the cake off the lid and onto a serving plate. Decorate the top and the plate with flowers. Serve now and wow!

Notes: Edible flowers are widely available online and at farmers' markets. Or look for flowers labeled "edible" in the produce section of the grocery store. Never eat flowers from a bouquet or that are not specifically sold as food. Lavender extract paste, such as Taylor & Colledge brand, is sold in specialty food shops, larger grocery stores, and online.

Store the cheesecake in the **JEL-RING** mold in the refrigerator.

PREP UP TO
2 DAYS AHEAD

SERVES 8 TO 12

Caramelized Pineapple Upside-Down Cake

- 4 tablespoons plus ½ cup unsalted butter, at room temperature
- ¼ cup packed dark brown sugar
- ¼ teaspoon ground cinnamon
- ¼ teaspoon ground ginger
- Pinch of ground nutmeg
- One 15-ounce can pineapple rings, drained, with 2 tablespoons juice reserved
- ⅔ cup superfine sugar (see Notes)
- 1 teaspoon pure vanilla extract
- 2 eggs, at room temperature
- 1 cup all-purpose flour
- 1 teaspoon baking powder
- ¼ teaspoon kosher salt
- Maraschino cherries, for garnish, (optional)

Baking a cake in a tart pan gives it a beautifully fluted edge and a larger surface area, perfect for thinner slices with the ideal balance of fragrant caramelized pineapple topping and cinnamony, gingery brown sugar. These flavors melt into the tender cake, transforming this old-fashioned dessert into a contemporary favorite.

1. Preheat the oven to 350°F. Place a 12-inch silicone tart form on a metal baking sheet.

2. In a medium bowl, using a handheld mixer, cream together 4 tablespoons of the butter, the brown sugar, cinnamon, ginger, and nutmeg on medium speed until pale brown and fluffy. Use a silicone spatula to spread the mixture in an even layer on the bottom of the tart form. Rinse the mixer beaters and the spatula and reserve.

3. Place a single pineapple ring in the center of the brown sugar layer, then arrange the remaining pineapple rings in a circle around the center ring.

4. Wipe out the bowl and add the remaining ½ cup butter and the superfine sugar to it. Using the mixer, beat together on medium speed until pale and fluffy. Add the vanilla and pineapple juice and beat until incorporated. Add the eggs one at a time, beating after each addition until incorporated.

5. In a small bowl, sift together the flour, baking powder, and salt. Using the silicone spatula, gently fold the flour mixture into the egg mixture until a thick batter forms and no white streaks remain.

6. Spoon the batter over the pineapple rings and gently spread to form a thin, even layer. Try not to move the pineapple rings.

7. Bake until a toothpick inserted into the center comes out clean, about 30 minutes. Allow the cake to cool in the form on a wire cooling rack for 20 minutes before inverting it onto a large serving plate. Garnish the pineapple centers with maraschino cherries, if desired. Enjoy now!

Notes: Superfine sugar is finely ground granulated sugar, so it dissolves more easily. You can make your own by pulverizing ⅔ cup granulated sugar in a blender.

Store the cake covered at room temperature.

PREP UP TO
1 WEEK AHEAD

SERVES 8 TO 10

Strawberry Crunch Ice Cream Bars

30 vanilla or strawberry creme sandwich cookies, finely crushed (about 4 cups)

6 tablespoons unsalted butter, melted

One 3-ounce package strawberry gelatin dessert powder

2 cups packed vanilla ice cream

2 cups packed strawberry ice cream

These strawberry-forward ice cream bars are serving summer neighborhood vibes—just supersized and (almost) homemade. Grab your favorite vanilla and strawberry ice creams and strawberry or vanilla creme cookies for fast assembly. This recipe is the perfect make-ahead treat for a birthday bash, poolside hang, or anywhere ice cream bars will be appreciated (so, everywhere).

1. Line the bottom and sides of an 11 by 7-inch freezer-safe container with one piece of compostable parchment paper (about 15 by 10¾ inches).

2. In a medium bowl, stir together 3 cups of the cookie crumbs, the butter, and ¼ cup of the gelatin powder until it's the consistency of wet sand. Press the mixture onto the bottom of the container to form an even crust. Place the container in the freezer for 30 minutes for the crust to harden. Meanwhile, let the vanilla ice cream soften.

3. Place the softened ice cream in a medium bowl and swirl it around with a large spoon until it's creamy and spreadable. Remove the container from the freezer and spread the vanilla ice cream in an even layer over the top of the crust. Return the container to the freezer for 30 minutes for the vanilla layer to harden. Meanwhile, let the strawberry ice cream soften and rinse the bowl and spoon.

4. Place the softened strawberry ice cream in the medium bowl and swirl it around with the spoon until it's creamy and spreadable. Remove the container from the freezer and spread the strawberry ice cream in an even layer over the frozen vanilla ice cream layer.

5. In a small bowl, stir together the remaining 1 cup cookie crumbs and remaining gelatin powder. Scatter the mixture evenly over the soft top layer of strawberry ice cream. Cover the container and freeze until hardened, at least 4 hours.

6. *To serve:* Remove the cover and invert the container onto a large cutting board. Wet a clean kitchen towel with hot water and drape it over the container. Let sit for 2 minutes. Remove the towel, lift the container, and voilà!—the ice cream mold will release with ease. Use your fingers and a spatula to quickly flip it over to reveal the topping. Cut into eight to ten bars and enjoy now!

Note: Store the bars covered in a freezer-safe container in the freezer.

For more than eighty years, the Tupperware brand has brought ingenuity and innovation into kitchens around the world—helping families save time, stretch their dollars, and discover joy in creating meals together. From pioneering designs that changed the way we store and serve food to clever solutions that continue to inspire today, our brand has always been about making life in the kitchen smarter, easier, more creative, and more connected. We hope the recipes and ideas within these pages spark your creativity, bring ease to your cooking, and help you make lasting memories around the table. Keep innovating, keep sharing, and keep creating the moments that truly matter.

With eight decades of love,
The Tupperware Kitchen

About the Contributors

The **TUPPERWARE** brand began in 1946 with the invention of unique preparation, storage, and serving containers for the kitchen and has evolved into so much more. With products originally sold almost exclusively by direct sales people from their homes and at parties, the Tupperware brand launched the concept of social selling. Over the last eighty years, Tupperware products have helped address food waste and empower women entrepreneurs in the growing gig economy.

THERESA GAMBACORTA is a writer and recipe developer. Her projects span from children's cooking to health and wellness as well as collaborations with chefs. She has co-authored such cookbooks as *The Elf on the Shelf Family Cookbook*, *Eat What Elephants Eat*, and *Sofreh*. She lives in Jersey City with her husband and son.

EVA KOLENKO is a food-centric photographer who has contributed her art and vision to more than 50 cookbooks. Based in Northern California, her passion for food extends beyond her Sonoma food studio to her home kitchen and garden, where you'll probably find her still in pajamas.

Tupperware

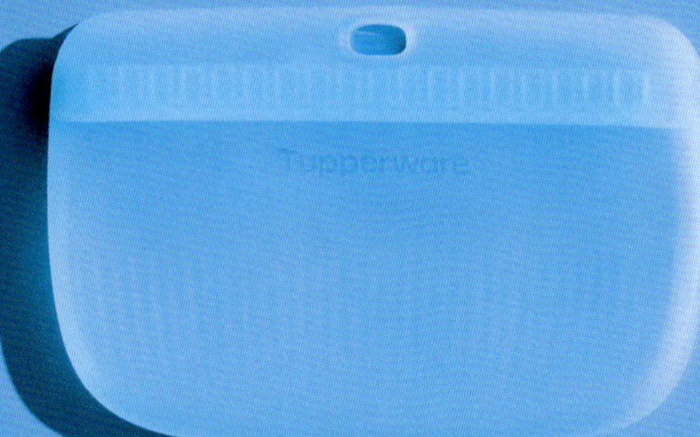
Tupperware

Tupperware
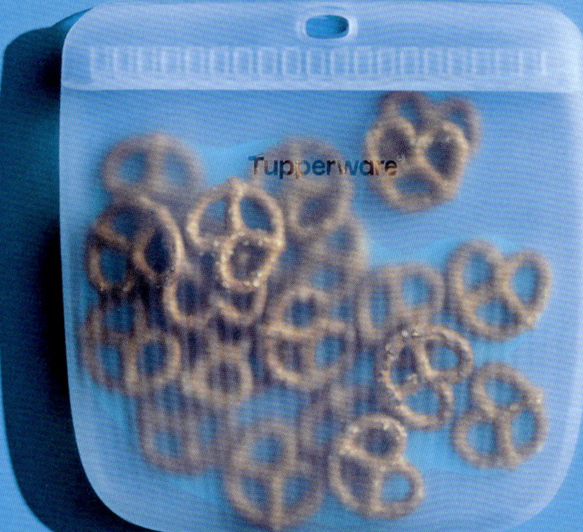
Tupperware

Tupperware

Note: *Italicized* pages refer to photos.

D

E

F

TEN SPEED PRESS
An imprint of the Crown Publishing Group
A division of Penguin Random House LLC
1745 Broadway | New York, NY 10019
tenspeed.com
penguinrandomhouse.com

Typefaces: Tupperware's Earl Tupper Sans, and The Northern Block's Eldwin Script and Eldwin Capitals.

Library of Congress Cataloging-in-Publication Data
Names: Gambacorta, Theresa author | Party US Operations LLC contributor Title: The Tupperware cookbook : Over 100 make-ahead recipes with low waste and high flavor / by Tupperware with Theresa Gambacorta. Identifiers: LCCN 2025016891 (print) | LCCN 2025016892 (ebook) | ISBN 9780593837443 hardcover | ISBN 9780593837450 ebook Subjects: LCSH: Make-ahead cooking | Food waste—Prevention | LCGFT: Cookbooks Classification: LCC TX652 .G344 2026 (print) | LCC TX652 (ebook) | DDC 641.5/55—dc23/eng/20250702
LC record available at
https://lccn.loc.gov/2025016891
LC ebook record available at
https://lccn.loc.gov/2025016892

Hardcover ISBN 978-0-593-83744-3
Ebook ISBN 978-0-593-83745-0

Acquiring editor: Molly Birnbaum
Project editor: Dena Rayess
Production editor: Sohayla Farman
Assistant editor: Gabby Ureña Matos
Designer: Francesca Truman
Art director: Emma Campion
Production designers: Mari Gill and Faith Hague
Production: Philip Leung
Food stylist: Natalie Drobny
Food stylist assistants: Carrie Beyer and Allison Fellion
Prop stylist: Genesis Vallejo
Digitech and photo retoucher: Eva Kolenko
Recipe developer: Theresa Gambacorta
Copy editor: Sharon Silva
Proofreaders: Adaobi Obi Tulton, Mark McCauslin, Robin Slutzky, and Tess Rossi
Indexer: Amy Hall
Marketer: Andrea Portanova

Manufactured in China

10 9 8 7 6 5 4 3 2 1

First Edition

Cover photographs: Eva Kolenko
Cover design: Francesca Truman
Cover art direction: Emma Campion

The authorized representative in the EU for product safety and compliance is Penguin Random House Ireland, Morrison Chambers, 32 Nassau Street, Dublin D02 YH68, Ireland, https://eu-contact.penguin.ie.